STARFALL
I Saved The Life Of A Space Alien

By

Albert Coe

Starfall - I Saved The Life Of A Space Alien
By Albert Coe

Additional material by Timothy Green Beckley and Sean Casteel

Published by Timothy Green Beckley
dba Inner Light/Global Communicatons

This Edition Copyright © 2021
by Inner Light/Global Communications

Revised Edition

Published in the United States of America By
Global Communications/Inner Light
11 East 30th Street 4R · New York, NY 10016

Staff Members
Timothy G. Beckley, Publisher
Carol Ann Rodriguez, Assistant to the Publisher
Sean Casteel, General Associate Editor
Tim R. Swartz, Graphics and Editorial Consultant
William Kern, Format, Layout and Graphics

Sign Up On The Web For Our Free Weekly Newsletter
and Mail Order Version of Conspiracy Journal
and Bizarre Bazaar
www.ConspiracyJournal.com

Order Hot Line: 1-646-331-6777

PayPal: MrUFO8@hotmail.com

CONTENTS

ILLUSTRATIONS
By Thomas Lulevitch

Dedication

I dedicate this book to Hazel Simpson whose understanding and cooperation have contributed, so deeply, to the inspiration of its structure. The beauty of thought will forever extol the virtue of womanhood as, from their hearts, flow the eternal breath of life.

—Albert Coe

Preface

"I am not an advocate for frequent changes in laws and constitutions, but laws and institutions must go hand in hand with the progress of the human mind. As that becomes more developed, more enlightened, as new discoveries are made, new truth discovered and manners and opinions change, with the change of circumstances, institutions must advance also to keep pace with the times. We might as well require a man to wear still the coat which fitted him while a boy, as civilized society to remain ever under the regimen of their barbarous ancestors."

—Thomas Jefferson

INTRODUCTION

The essence of these famous words have reverberated throughout the passage of time, yet man seems loath or unable to cast off the tentacles of habit which he builds over the centuries and  is more inclined to try to wedge or fit advancing knowledge, newly discovered truth, into his set form pattern of cherished ideal or outmoded tradition. The intent of this book is to bring a fuller comprehension, a more concise definition of the evolutionary necessity of readjustment, by an introduction to a race of people whose origins, although foreign to our solar system, are not unlike us in physical appearance and who, from their own tiny niche of this infinite whole, have established a certain truer conformity to these ideals.

The latter part of their history, covering a time span of some 20,000 years, has at times, been fraught with death, disaster and heartbreak. But this frustration of adversity, compiled through the diversification in a sequence of natural law and the rebuff of fellow humans, did not undermine the fundamental concepts of a philosophy based on the broad footing of knowledge and formulated under a premise that "being" is beauty, combining love, brotherhood and compassion.

They endowed to our ancient ancestors, their intelligence, in a short lived colonization under these precepts, that concluded in mass slaughter and near destruction of the planet through our insatiable compulsion to conquest. But, undaunted, they once again knit a shattered populace into the brotherhood which had never accepted the reaction of defeatism, nor stooped to a reciprocal action of violence.

Now, with our reentry into research of the atom, probing a

more refined instrument of obliteration and bearing in mind the horrible memory of a bygone age, they sent a group of one hundred observers to evaluate an advance in destructive forces and in determining our potential of shattering our planet. We are indebted to them for efficiently fabricating a neutralizing screen, encompassing earth, comprising the inner status of what is now known as the "Van Allen Belt." This action was a forethought to counteract a possible cataclysm through a chain reaction of the hydrogen atom, if or when we may lose control of these devices, thus guarantying a chance of limited survival.

The creating of this screen and its later refinement has given rise to the myriad "Fireballs" and "Unidentified Flying Objects," which have mystified modern man for the past twenty-two years, just as the legendary awareness of a "different" presence has bewildered our forbearers, for almost ten thousand years.

After the energizing of this "screen" a group of these men sought to institute an oral contact, through debate, with the aim of instilling a thought trend to offset the mental shackles which bind us so tightly to archaic precept and to paraphrase the aptly coined words of Jefferson, "Trying to fit the grown man into his childhood coat."

Its parallel forever plagues us, as throughout our lives we labor under the paradox of trying to balance the old world of superstition and theory with the new world of progress and science, a series of six letters were formulated, even though their request for debate drew only the emptiness of silence. The impelling impulse that created the thought of these letters stemmed from the hope that it may awaken a desire of reappraisal. They had hoped, through our own volition, to lend impetus to an overhaul of doctrine.

It was their desire that with this incorporation of factual science and its clearer understanding of universal motivation, to draw these now completely divorced ends of fact and theory into a more compatible skein of rational philosophy. They fear now, that without stabilization, our apparent aimless drift into a "Nuclear Age," burdened under the stigma of warfare, unreasonable proliferation, starvation and the chaos of conflicting ideology may only lead to the gulf of "oblivion."

In full realization that tales of "Flying Saucers," "little green men," prancing about the countryside and fantastic journeys to such outlandish places as Jupiter, Saturn and even the fantasy of a flight through the Sun by a supposed selected few, have been the "butt" of many jokes and subjected to all manner of ridicule, there is a basic undercurrent of truth which runs through each story, each sighting. The great impetus to mystery, to conjecture and the grotesque materializations of imagination, stems from lack of their true identity and determination of purpose that, to date, has never been clearly or logically defined. The return to earth of physical, "rational men" is an irrefutable fact and they came with a definite problem to solve.

Their mission originated without inclusion of knowledgeable contact with us or a "national" desire of social intercourse with our races. The method used to infiltrate was quite unusual and not in strict concurrence with our established laws and they utilized the security of secrecy, to work unhampered, in proving or to disprove their grave concern, that centered only on our ability to construct devices of destruction. They left nothing to chance, as their interest concentrated in a study of possible counteractives should we reach a point that may unleash one, or a combination of nature's own explosive capabilities.

In 1904 they paved the way for one hundred of their specially trained observers and infiltrated them as small groups of technicians in every major country of earth. Their job was to watch and evaluate each step of our scientific advancement. The later "prolific" appearance of the U.F.O. is contemporary to our research, in atoms for bombs, as they set in motion the conclusion of years of study to offset the probability of a "runaway" nuclear device triggering the detonation of the greatest bornb of all times, Earth itself.

The presentation of this story and its plot are probably as unorthodox as the material of its structure. Still, through their own determination, a cloak of secrecy has not been shed and I cannot offer a concrete proof. Their willingness to institute a series of debates was a fact and after reading this book, only the dictates of your mind may judge the authenticity of the remarkable story that it has to tell.

It opens with an adventure, in 1920, of two carefree boys on a canoe trip through the wilds of Canada; a chance meeting with one of this group of technicians, long before "Flying Saucers" and their unrealistic buildup were even a remote conception of thought. It expands in the history of two races of men, born on worlds light years apart, to eventually briefly intertwine and then again to separate, planets apart.

I, Albert Coe, was one of these two boys who had the good fortune to assist this "stranger," in a time of need and for forty-six years have honored a pledge, made to him, at this initial meeting in the forest. Only recently have I been released from the honor bond of this pledge and granted the leniency to compose this book in the hope that it may clarify the motivation of a "mystery" race. Their only desire is to live in the peace and beauty of nature's unfolding wonders, as, through their own unique philosophy, they have welded "love and compassion" into this universal skein. Intelligence never seeks to force its will on others, but if a seed will grow, through its own volition, perhaps the fruit of its wisdom may someday replace the weeds of brutality from all of humanity's races.

There is no intent of this book to proclaim that "God" is dead, and quite to the contrary gives far greater scope, a more expansive understanding of the supreme creative power in a Universe. However, it does take issue with the egoism of man that has inspired an assumption of being created from a very special clay, in the image of his God, and under this impression stands alone, above and beyond all the vast wonders of creation; the untold billions of galaxies, with their suns, planets and life forms relegated as jewels sprinkled in a sky to light his way by day or by night.

As long as one new life appears, one tiny spark shines in a darkened sky, "God," the creative power of a universe is not dead.

—The Author

Foreword

THE LEGEND OF ALBERT COE
KING OF THE "UFO REPEATERS"
By Sean Casteel
Notes by Timothy Green Beckley

One of the most fascinating – and difficult to analyze – aspects of the UFO phenomenon is the apparent non-randomness of sightings and the effects those sightings have on those who witness them. Often a long chain of events begins for the witness after a sighting, events fraught with various synchronicities, time distortions and lingering, newly discovered PSI abilities like telepathy and psychokinesis.

Beginning with Kenneth Arnold's 1947 sighting, a UFO encounter was considered to be something akin to being struck by lightning: it was completely involuntary and extremely unlikely to happen to someone a second time. But as the contactee movement of the 1950s began to gather strength, a different understanding began to emerge. Some people claimed to have ongoing relationships with the flying saucer occupants, and the otherworldly interlopers were even willing to pose for a few photos as well.

UFO publicist and publisher Timothy Green Beckley has collected a string of contact experiences where, once having established some form of communications with an otherworldly being – or beings – an ongoing relationship seems to have been established which can last for several years, and sometimes an entire lifetime. "Such an ongoing stellar 'correspondence' is rare, but it does happen," the editor of the now defunct newsstand publication, "UFO Review," cautiously points out. "I guess we all know that the most famous contactee of them all, George Adamski, professed to have connected with his Venusian cohort Orthon over a period of many years. I guess you could say they were cosmic homies of sorts."

It was a "chance encounter" of his own as a teenager that brought Beckley to the point where he has decided to publish a very rare manuscript pertaining to a contact experience – perhaps the earliest on record having taken place in modern times, specifically in 1920.

Tim establishes his reasons for issuing a book that he admits may have only a limited appeal, mostly among hardcore fans of the UFO contactee movement.

"Living in the suburbs of New Jersey, between New York City and Philadelphia, had its problems as far as TV and radio reception goes. I would race home to tune into Dick Clark's 'American Bandstand' which, in those early days of the program, was only being broadcast locally out of Philly. I was anxious to watch the guys and girls gyrate to the likes of Chuck Berry's 'Sweet Little Sixteen,' and Jerry Lee Lewis' 'Great Balls of Fire.' But mostly all we got was snow on the screen. Forget about Chubby Checker's 'Lets Twist Again,' as no amount of twisting of the rabbit ears would bring the picture in clearer."

Beckley also heard that there were certain radio stations "out and about" that were broadcasting regular shows on UFOs that he just had to hear. He was gaining an irrational interest in flying saucers, as they were still being called. In particular, he wanted to tune into the "UFOlogy Round Table," hosted by Earl J. Neff out of Cleveland, Ohio's KYW studios. It was a necessity if he was to survive those early teenage years and turn into the gentleman scholar he is today.

"I guess my parents got tired of me bitching and moaning as they had a very high directional antenna placed on the roof which cut down on the crackling of the AM radio so I could listen to Long John Nebel undisturbed. And by that time Dick Clark was being simulcast and the black and white picture was as good as you were going to get. High definition was a long ways off. Anyway, I got rid of the white noise on the radio long enough to hear Earl Neff read a post card I had sent in asking a question of his UFO-minded panel. I believe that would have been 1966 or thereabouts."

As Beckley recalls, just about every major station had an all-night talk show host and a lot of them were delving into UFOs as they realized that the topic had made WOR's Long John Nebel the toast of Manhattan from midnight to dawn.

"I can't recall offhand the station's call letters or the forgotten – to me at least – all-night talk show host who livened up the Philadelphia airwaves, but it was no cheese steak happenstance that I would tune in on my jazzed up radio receiver to the various stations I knew were talking about UFOs. One evening a particular guest intrigued me. Albert Coe claimed in what appeared to be all sincerity to have saved the life of an alien during a camping trip.

Albert Coe was a teenager on a trip to the mountains of Canada. It was in June 1920. They were to drift down the river in a canoe. Sometimes they had to carry the canoe over their heads to reach the next stretch of navigable river. One late evening Albert heard a faraway cry for help, while his friend was further downstream.

In a narrow cleft/gap, was a young man fallen, critically hurt, and not able to come out by himself. But Albert was then able to bring him out. He was clothed in a peculiar, silver gray, tight jumper-type garment – almost like silk. A small instrument panel was under the chest.

He said he was not canoeing, but had a plane nearby, and was fishing, but his equipment was really odd. Likewise his tale that he had a plane nearby. He was severely injured, but was reluctant to let Albert see his "plane." But at last, he had to let Albert help him to his "plane," as he could hardly walk on his own. But only if he agreed not to tell anyone of what he would then see.

He had expected to see a conventional craft of some sort, but instead he was witness to a round silver disc on three legs standing in the wilderness. It stood four to five feet from the ground. No windows. Albert wondered how he could see out.

As it turns out Albert was to meet up with this individual numerous times under a variety of circumstances. He was so human-looking that he was able to walk amongst us undetected.

"For some reason I felt compelled to write Albert Coe," recalls Beckley, "in care of the station and express my interest in his alleged experiences. I was really fishing for more information. Lo and behold if a couple of weeks later I didn't receive a thick manuscript in a black folder that came through the mail. While he hadn't published his story in book form, he was circulating a few carbon copies of his eventually-to-be-printed manuscript. The copy is still in my files – somewhere! He had no problem with it being reprinted and circulated. He wasn't out for fame nor money."

The manuscript has sat collecting dust over numerous decades forgotten by Beckley, until one of his longtime friends in the UFO field, Mindy Gerber, refreshed his memory by sending a pdf version of the manuscript someone had typed out years ago and then had a few hard covered copies printed.

"The story hearkens to the bygone days of the UFO era," Beckley muses. "In fact, supposedly all this transpired before Adamski, Fri and Van Tassel had come forth with their communications with stellar visitors." Beckley felt it was time to reprint the book along with this new introduction so that Coe's experiences would not be lost to the world.

And while Tim G. B. acknowledges that Albert's experiences are unique even for a "UFO repeater," because the same alien persisted in communicating with the experiencer throughout his life, which is somewhat rare, there is at least one other contactee who has been in the "gunsights" of one particular alien.

ALONG COMES WOODY DERENBERGER
AND INRID COLD

It doesn't take much for the average person's life to spiral out of control. If Woodrow Derenberger had been anyplace else on the night of November 2, 1966, chances are almost a million to one that his life as a traveling salesman would remain as placid as one could expect for someone living in rural West Virginia during this period in the late Sixties," or so states Beckley as he posts some more revelations, this one from his article published in Phyllis Galde's illustrious publication "Fate Magazine." Beckley's piece is called A STAR-STUDDED GUIDE TO THE TOP TEN UFO CONTACTEES OF ALL TIME.

"But no, as it turns out, Woodrow Derenberger was caught in a sudden downpour, so he slowed his truck down as he was leaving a sales meeting in Marietta, Ohio He had driven that stretch of Highway 1-77 back home to Mineral Wells, WV so many times that it had become a mundane task. He knew he was going to be late for supper, and he surely was, as his life was altered that night like no one, certainly Mr. Derenberger, could ever have expected. Cars were passing him, not concerned about the wet pavement. Suddenly, out of nowhere, a strange light appeared to pass over his vehicle. A strange ship landed on the embankment of an abandoned stretch of blacktop, a door slid open and a human-like being approached our witness in the dead of night.

"A rather brief conversation ensued. The stranger asked what the lights were off in the distance – a city it was explained, and there was some banter about the passing of time, and our miscalculation of it. The ship didn't stay long, though Woody was told that he would be contacted in the future – which he most certainly was!

"When Woody returned home, his wife noticed it looked like her husband had seen a ghost (perhaps he had!). Slowly she pulled the story of his otherworldly encounter from him and somehow the local TV station was called and Derenberger found himself thrust in the spotlight – for better or worse. And you know in UFOlogy which way the guideposts point up ahead.

"Woody had never concerned himself with things like UFOs, had hardly heard of them and could not imagine making contact with an alien pilot who became a common fixture in the family's household, so much so that he frequently came in for supper The spaceman eventually identified himself as Indrid Cold and said that he was from the planet Lanulous. Woody's backyard became an alien 'stronghold,' with ships buzzing around all over the place. Some folks waited for the arrival of the ETs, wanting to hunt them down with good ole Southern buckshot, while others wished to welcome their newfound friends from outer space, though no corn bread was offered. Among his supporters was a local psychiatrist whom Derenberger had gone to for counseling. Turns out the shrink had turned into a contactee himself and ended up verifying what the West Virginian had been claiming all along. And of course the doctor managed to add his own spin to the case at hand.

"Yes, there were plenty of spacemen afoot in the hills of the Mountain State.

"To take matters further, the traveling salesman for a sewing machine firm claimed that in 1967 he had actually traveled to their home planet in the far away Ganymede system and that the Landulocians were peace-loving people who wanted to set up an exchange program with our world, only to be continually rebuffed by the government. They also were nudists, as apparently are many space people. For cosmic joy!

"Says one source close to the late contactee: 'Woodrow's wife was terrified and stated that these beings were much like us: traveled in everyday cars, dressed in everyday clothes, but were not human in origin. There was even one time where Mr. Derenberger disappeared for six months and said he was with Indrid Cold. This is what members of his family actually believed. He would also receive mental messages from his long distant friend. They would come on suddenly and leave piercing migraine headaches.'

"Woody Derenberger rose to national prominence with the release of John Keel's 'Mothman Prophecies' book, which was eventually made into a movie starring Richard Gere. Keel claimed to have received phone calls from Indrid Cold while staying in a Point Pleasant, WV, motel when no one knew he was even in town to check out stories of the elusive Mothman, a winged creature which was often tied in with Woody's story. That story also included tales of the sinister Men in Black.

"Woody eventually wrote a book, 'Visitors From Landulous.' He lectured at my psychic center in Manhattan and even fell into Witch Hazel's – yes that was the name of the very voluptuous occultist – coffin in the dark. But that's another story meant only for midnight gossip.

"Indrid Cold eventually broke up Woody's marriage, and

there is some talk that spouses were swapped due to the otherworldly circumstances of what was going on day and night on and around the Derenberger property, especially out back where the saucers continued to land, and were being witnessed by those who came to gawk, or the few who wished to seek the eternal truth about our UFO visitors.

"WD passed away in 1990, and while in ill health his daughter has attempted to carry on with Woody's legacy. In 'Beyond Lanulos,' Taunia Derenberger continues the story begun by her father more than 50 years ago, when he famously encountered the spaceman, Indrid Cold, on Interstate 77 outside of Mineral Wells, West Virginia.

"The Appalachians have never had it so good!" writes Tim, as he concludes his sermon on Woody in a matter-of-fact tone.

Those wishing a more thorough overview of Derenberger's lifetime of encounters should check out one of our favorite blogs, PhantomsAndMonsters.com – in particular their post for July 21, 2020 for "Lessons Learned," pertaining to Woody's extended proceedings with Mr. Cold. Unlike in the case of Albert Coe, all things were not hunky-dory during his interplanetary relationship.

THE CAMERA DOESN'T LIE!

This all brings to mind – going full circle – that group within the UFO community that we identify as "UFO repeaters," a phrase that brings to mind a book Tim Beckley published several years ago. The book is called *"UFO Repeaters: Seeing Is Believing! The Camera DoesnÕt Lie!"* As the title implies, it is chock full of photos by people who were repeatedly given the opportunity to take aim and shoot UFOs with both still and mo-tion picture cameras.

Many of the photos in *"UFO Repeaters"* are quite dramatic and will elicit gasps of wonderment even from people already jaded by years of studying the subject. No real attempt is made in the book to debate whether the photos are authentic. The late alien abduction research pioneer, Budd Hopkins, once said that we will always have difficulty in assessing the "truth" of a UFO photo because even one that photo analysis experts could not completely debunk would still look like something conjured by Hollywood through the special effects department. Hopkins also said that all we can really be sure of is ourselves, meaning that we should study the UFO phenomenon by picking it up from the human end of the stick.

Which "*UFO Repeaters*" also manages to accomplish when it tells the personal stories of several of the contactees themselves who became shutterbugs for the flying saucers. How and why these contactees were "chosen" for their mission of revealing the alien presence through the lens of the camera remains unknown, but some elusive factor unites them all.

In his introduction, publisher and author Beckley grapples with that and similar issues. For example, he writes, "Is it the individual – the UFO Repeater – who is solely responsible for the images on the film or video? Do they possess some sort of tracking device – an implant – that the aliens use as a homing apparatus to keep in touch with their representatives? Are some of the images 'psychic' in nature? Are they manifested by the Repeaters themselves? Sort of like a poltergeist event? Or perhaps it's that the locale is a 'hotspot' that draws the UFOs in, and anyone could be standing in this location and capture weird images which are indisputably NOT anything within the realm of the 'normal.' Perhaps it is a combination of all of the above."

DIANE TESSMAN

"And of course Diane Tessman's lifelong meetings with her 'special one,'" Beckley adds, "whom she identifies as 'Tibus,' are well known among our readership. We have helped promote Diane's experiences, which began when she was a young girl living in Iowa. Her second meeting that she recalls took place in a rather remote cabin while her parents were away. Dr. Leo Sprinkle, a psychologist on the faculty of the University of Wyoming, helped nudge along the recollection of her contacts through hypnosis, but she remembers many details on her own. Tibus speaks through her to this very day.

"You can read more about her experiences in '*The Transformation Of Diane Tessman*.' Tibus and Diane have established a bonding companionship and he has taught her a great deal about the mysteries of time and space."

STELLA LANSING

The veteran paranormal journalist Tim R. Swartz begins the book by getting down to cases. For example, Stella Lansing of Palmer, Massachusetts, who had the strange ability to "call down" UFOs and photograph them using both still and film cameras. Many of the images were not apparent when Stella took the pictures but instead seemed to spontaneously appear on film. She claimed to have experienced seeing strange little men and creatures, hearing voices speaking out of nowhere, suffering an electric shock administered by a "shimmering figure," and a craft surfacing from underwater.

It was Beckley himself who gave Stella her first brush with fame when she came to a UFO convention Beckley helped to organize in 1967. She showed Beckley a series of home movies that had captured what he called "eerie, phantom-like phenomena." One of Stella's films seemed to show four occupants visible through a window on the spacecraft. Other 8mm films contained clock-like patterns of light that would overlap the frames, something considered to be optically impossible.

Stella talked about her experiences with author Brad Steiger for his book *Gods of Aquarius*."

"I don't know if they came from another planet," Stella said, "or if they live right within our dimension, or if they're interdimensional – or maybe they're living somewhere on Earth that we haven't discovered yet. But whatever it is I do, it's as if I'm programmed in some way to sense the need to take pictures of UFOs. I feel a sudden compulsion to pick up my camera, a sudden urgency to really grab that camera. I sense that maybe I am being 'told,' but I don't even know – I'm not consciously aware. When I snap the shutter, that's when I get my pictures of UFOs or entities. Something is making me do it without my being aware of it. I'm only aware of it after it's happened."

Stella continued to see and photograph UFOs as well as to keep detailed notes even after interest in her work had long since faded. She was always willing to talk about her experiences, but, right up to her death in 2012, she remained mystified by her own strange abilities. Nevertheless, the media always enjoyed telling her story, such as the ever popular TV series "Unsolved Mysteries." She lives on in this clip available on YouTube by following this link: https://www.youtube.com/edit?video_id=5WF1LDn8pz8&video_referrer=watch

DOROTHY IZATT

Swartz also writes about a Canadian woman named Dorothy Izatt who photographed an amazing array of UFOs. What is so incredible about Dorothy's films are the "one-frame" images that pop up unexpectedly, showing streaks of light and other luminous objects.

"It all started when she saw a bright object hovering in the sky above her house," Swartz writes. "Dorothy went out onto her balcony with a flashlight and tried signaling the UFO, which, to her amazement, signaled back. When she told her friends about her experience, no one believed her. So she went out and bought a Keystone XL 200 Super-8 movie camera and started filming. The results were more than 600 reels of film that skeptics, right from the very beginning, have said were faked. But, if she is faking them, photo experts have yet to figure out how."

Dorothy's films have been seen widely on television shows like "Unsolved Mysteries" and "Sightings." She calls the UFO occupants "light beings," not aliens, because "we are aliens, too."

Dorothy said that, from the very beginning, she could tell when a UFO was near and that she would be compelled to get her camera and film them. She later learned that she was being directed by telepathic communications from the extraterrestrials.

"You talk mind-to-mind," she explained. "They can pick up your thoughts, and I have the ability to pick up theirs, too. There are all different types of beings. Some are like us. You wouldn't be able to tell the difference if they walked among us. Some are different, but down here on this Earth we are all different, too."

Oddly, some people can see the aliens when she points them out, but others can't. She feels her own ability to see them is the result of a special sense she possesses. When she wants to make contact, all she has to do is concentrate and they appear. Dorothy says she was born with this "sense" and that she shares it with other members of her family.

"Even though many UFO researchers try to ignore the psychic component of UFOs," Swartz writes, "the rejection of this key element will only contribute to the continuing confusion that surrounds the phenomenon. Since the 1940s, UFOs have become synonymous with spaceships and extraterrestrials. However, this interpretation is far too simplistic and probably reflects modern social belief structures more than science fact."

BETTY HILL

The UFO abduction of Betty and Barney Hill has been well-documented in books such as the "Interrupted Journey," by journalist John Fuller, and "Captured! The Betty and Barney Hill UFO Experience," coauthored by Kathleen Marden (Betty's niece) and longtime UFO researcher Stanton Friedman.

In 1961, the Hills underwent what would become a template for alien abduction that has been repeated for other people countless times in the years since. The couple was taken from their car as they drove from Canada to their home in New Hampshire, brought onboard a landed UFO, medically examined, and then returned to their car with no conscious memory of the strange events that had just taken place. The Hills would not recover their memories until a few years later when a Boston psychiatrist led them through the process of regressive hypnosis. The use of hypnosis to unearth the buried memories of an encounter would become another commonplace aspect of the aftermath of the alien abduction experience.

Although the Hill case is a familiar one to most in the UFO community, what is not so widely-known is that, after the 1961 encounter, Betty and her side of the family experienced not only additional UFO sightings but also unusual harassments in the form of house break-ins, weird telephone calls and paranormal activity. A scientific research team convinced Betty to take part in an experiment to see whether she could reestablish contact with her captors. The goal was to vector in a craft to land in the vicinity of Betty's home. Betty attempted to reach out to the UFO occupants via verbal and telepathic messages. The UFOs did indeed begin to appear shortly thereafter, followed by a spate of paranormal activity that included household items flying off of shelves, doors opening and closing on their own, and light orbs darting through the air.

Betty wrote that, "These things are happening to Barney and me as well as to most of my relatives, but they have also been witnessed by other people who were present. We do not believe in ghosts but we do believe in space travel and life on other planets. So we wonder if these space travelers might have the ability to be 'unseen' to us."

Many of her admirers do not realize that Betty had a "favorite spot" that she visited frequently in order to try and communicate with and "bring down" those beings that had taken her and Barney away so many years previously. Her efforts resulted in a number of odd photographs that she added to her personal collection of memorabilia but which had skeptics wagging their tongues in annoyed disbelief.

HOWARD MENGER

Howard Menger's story is the kind you hope is true simply for the reassurance it offers about the nature of the UFO occupants. Howard encountered the kind of beautiful, loving creatures that seem to come right out of a children's storybook about good spirits taking a young boy on a fantastic adventure in a kind of colorful "wonderland."

Howard was born in 1922 in Brooklyn, New York. When Howard was ten, his parents moved the family to a spacious, rustic homestead in rural New Jersey. Howard and his brother would explore the nearby pastures and hills, where the paranormal activity soon commenced. On several occasions, the youths maintained, they were cornered by weird objects resembling Buck Rogers-like spacecraft that appeared over the tree line and sent the boys scampering away in fear. At one point, a ten-foot diameter disc landed close to Howard and his brother while another larger object hovered overhead, as if to gauge the boys' reaction to the landed craft.

Little by little, Howard, being more "sensitive" than his brother, started to venture out into the pastures and meadowlands on his own. He easily made friends with the fauna there, like squirrels and rabbits, and was particularly attracted to a specific spot near a slow-running stream that ran in the back of the family home. On a bright, sunny day in 1932, he saw something there that would change his life forever.

"There, sitting on a rock by the brook," Howard said, "was the most exquisite woman my young eyes had ever beheld! The warm sunlight caught the highlights of her long, golden hair as it cascaded around her face and shoulders. The curves of her lovely body were delicately contoured, revealed through the translucent material of her clothing, which reminded me of the habit that skiers wear."

In spite of the woman's sudden and strange appearance out of nowhere, Howard was not frightened. He was instead "overcome by an overwhelming sense of wonderment" that made him freeze in his tracks. He felt a tremendous surge of warmth and love emanating from the woman and he approached her as one would an old friend or loved one.

The woman called him by name and said she had come a long way to see him and speak to him.

"She said she knew where I had come from," Howard recalled, "and what my purpose would be here on Earth. She and her people had observed me for a long time and in ways I would not quickly understand. When she spoke of her 'people,' I still could not understand they were from another planet. I seemed to be encompassed by the very glow, almost visible, that emanated from her presence. I have often tried to describe it as like seeing a Technicolor movie in three dimensions and being a part of the action in the film."

Again, the mysterious woman called Howard by name and said, "We are contacting our own," words that Howard said would bring more joy and take on more meaning as he grew older. "It is no fault of yours, Howard, that you cannot understand everything. Do not worry," she comforted him. Then her face took on an air of sadness, and she spoke of grave changes, destruction and torment that would move as a dark cloud over the country and the world. Before departing, the woman said he would see her again but it might not be for a long time.

Howard returned to the same spot again often but the lady never reappeared.

Later, while an adult serving in the army, Howard was on vacation in Mexico when he encountered a man with shoulder-length blond hair sitting in a cab that Howard had just hailed. The blond man spoke to him without moving his lips, telepathically, and told Howard that he had been selected for a series of contacts with the aliens.

The alien warned Howard that his life might be in danger during his military service but it would never be necessary for him to kill anyone. This prophecy later came true when Howard was attacked by a Japanese soldier who came at him with a razor-sharp bayonet, cutting a hole in Howard's tent in the middle of the night. Howard began firing at the enemy soldier, wounding him, but not mortally.

Howard would bump into his space friends nearly everywhere he went. They looked human enough, but there was just something odd about their appearance – something a bit "off" perhaps – that convinced him these visitors meant what they said when they claimed to be from other planets. They intimated to Howard that he had been selected to become a contactee because he had some of the same benevolent qualities about him that they had.

After the war, Howard returned to New Jersey and his contacts increased. He met them in his home as well as outdoors in several remote rendezvous spots where he had been told to go. On a number of occasions, he carried a camera with him to record some of their aerial activities. He even managed to get some still photos of the beings approaching him, backlit by the brightly illuminated exterior of their ship and creating eerie shadows.

As the years went on, Howard would gain fame as a contactee, perhaps second only to George Adamski, and would write a book called "From Outer Space To You" that remains a classic in its genre. Though controversy continues about whether Howard was part of a government "silence" group intent on muddying the waters regarding the truth about the flying saucer phenomenon, his many photos are still with us, and a goodly selection of those are featured in "UFO Repeaters."

Coauthor Tim Beckley admits that he is predisposed to believing in Howard's fanciful stories because "he was such a charming individual . . . the type of guy who doesn't seem capable of lying to you." Beckley says he lived down the road from Howard and often heard chatter from others who had "seen and heard things" on and around Howard's property, despite the fact that they didn't really hook up with Howard himself. His rural neighbors pretty much kept to themselves but had witnessed enough to be capable of verifying some of the strange happenings said to have transpired in the apple orchard out back of Howard's Highbridge, New Jersey, home.

PAUL VILLA

Like the legendary Swiss contactee, Billy Meier, Paul Villa was an unassuming gentleman of modest means who happened to capture some striking UFO photos. Paul had no axe to grind and no desire for publicity or fame. As so often happens in the world of UFO encounters, Paul did not find the flying saucer phenomenon; it found him.

Paul told UFO investigators that he would receive a telepathic message telling him to be at a certain location, usually somewhere near his home in Albuquerque, New Mexico. When he arrived at the designated place, the aliens would essentially "pose" for him while he took photos with a Japanese-made camera and standard Kodak film.

The result of those efforts is a beautiful series of full color photos depicting the flying saucers in all their glory. According to UFO researcher Wendelle Stevens, Paul's photos are quite sharp compared to most photos of that era, which was the 1960s through the 1970s. The image size of the saucers is large enough to show good detail and the fact that Paul's truck is in the foreground of some of the photos provides a known object with which to compare the size of the saucer and to judge its distance away from the camera.

Paul was born in 1916 of Native American/Spanish descent. He did not complete the tenth grade but had a good working knowledge of mathematics, physics, electricity and mechanics and was particularly gifted at detecting defects in engines and generators.

In 1953, while he was employed by the Department of Water and Power in Los Angeles, Paul encountered a man about seven feet tall who called him by name and could read his mind as well as knowing a great many facts about Paul's past. The spaceman invited Paul to come aboard a metallic-looking, disc-shaped object floating on the water nearby and Paul agreed to go.

For Paul, the aliens were entirely human-looking, though more uniformly attractive than Earth people and definitely more refined in face and form. They took Paul on a tour of the saucer and said they are here on a friendly mission to help Earth people. As his contact experiences continued through the years, Paul was eventually invited to photograph the ships. The aliens flew their craft slowly and hovered as Paul snapped away. In the mid-1960s, the photos began to draw the interest of flying saucer organizations, who debated the pictures' authenticity and even at times tried to prove Paul to be a fraud.

The photos Paul took are breathtaking to look at and do appear to show genuine flying saucers set against lovely desert scenery. There are varying types of ships from photo to photo, which is consistent with UFO witness accounts since the 1940s and has led some analysts to think we are being visited by several different alien races and civilizations.

The notoriety that came with being chosen to take the photos did not make life easy for Paul, however. When he stopped at a local tavern one evening on his way home from work and sat sipping a beer, a stranger walked up and drew Paul's blood with a punch in nose. His assailant called Paul crazy for "talking to spacemen." On top of that, unwelcome curiosity seekers would descend on his family home and take "souvenirs" with them when they left. All the various forms of harassment necessitated relocating his family on several occasions.

Paul died in 1980 at age 64. Some of his photos were never made public, including a series that was reportedly taken on another planet. We may never know everything the UFO occupants revealed to Paul, but the idea that there is further photographic evidence of his to be seen is certainly a tantalizing one.

PERHAPS THE PHOTOS ARE FREELY GIVEN?

"UFO Repeaters" also includes photos by and the personal histories of other people who were selected to photograph flying saucers and, on occasion, their occupants. Ellen Crystall, Ed Walters, Joe Ferriere, Marc Brinkerhoff – the list goes on – were all at one time "brought into the fold," so to speak, and produced a continual stream of photos that implies that there is some kind of mutual trust and, in some cases, an apparently loving relationship with the beings flying the ships at work here.

Why are these Repeaters granted this kind of privileged status with the UFO occupants? Why do the aliens seem to cancel the "terror factor" in certain cases and instead establish a caring, compassionate bond with some experiencers that continues throughout the mortal's entire life? The vagaries of how these alien choices are made continue to elude us.

But, in the meantime, Global Communications can offer you this: a book that takes the stories behind these photographs and the people that took them basically at face value. There is no reason to doubt the photos' authenticity, and many have long ago passed muster with photo analysis experts who were forced to concede that – whether or not there really IS an alien presence – the photos themselves were not the result of tampering or tricks.

The aliens have chosen to reveal their existence in many ways since Kenneth Arnold's 1947 sighting started the ball rolling in the modern era. If this is so, why would occasional genuine photos not be part of that overall mix? Why would the UFO occupants withhold that kind of verification if they were willing to provide so many other forms of proof and confirmation?

But we are just beginning our tale of cosmic wonderment and will commence forthwith in our next installment to continue revealing the truth about the UFO Repeaters and their sincere efforts to document the reality of the unknown through the eye of the camera.

As the book's title enthuses: Seeing is believing!

SUGGESTED READING

· UFO REPEATERS! – SEEING IS BELIEVING – THE CAMERA DOESN'T LIE

· THE SAUCERS SPEAK – CALLING ALL OCCUPANTS OF INTERPLANETARY CRAFT

· THE AUTHENTIC BOOK OF ULTRA-TERRESTRIAL CONTACTS: FROM THE SECRET ALIEN FILES OF UFO RESEARCHER TIMOTHY GREEN BECKLEY

· MR. UFO'S SECRET FILES – OUR YOUTUBE CHANNEL WITH OVER 400 INTERVIEWS

And Visit:
· EXPLORING THE BIZARRE, KCORRADIO.COM, EVERY THURSDAY AT 10 P.M. EASTERN WITH COHOST TIM SWARTZ

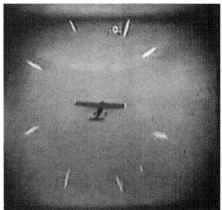

Deformed faces and clock-like light patterns were among the inter-dimensional images photographed by Stella Lansing.

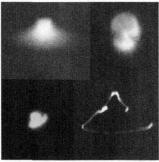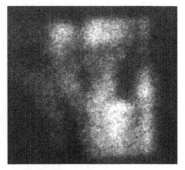

Canada's Dorothy Izatt has photographed an amazing array of UFOs.

Howard Menger said space beings were emerging from UFOs that landed out back in his apple orchard.

Paul Villa has taken some remarkable photos of UFOs hovering over his truck as well as a photo of a ship preparing to touch down on tripod landing gears.

Diane Tessman has had an exceptional friend throughout her life. She calls her "special one" -- Tibus.

Woody Derenberger's daughter holds photo of her dad.

People From Venus Live Among Us— This Man's Known Them For Years

ALBERT COE

By ART BENTLEY
MIDNIGHT Staff Writer

Albert Coe is slender of build, medium of height, moderate of tone and has a good friend from Venus.

And not Venus de Milo, either. Venus, da planet.

"I'm not trying to make you believe me," he tells the skeptics who listen to his lectures. "There's no way I can prove it. They're very elusive as far as letting anyone know who they are."

So how come Albert Coe, a 72-year-old retired engineer who lives quietly in Philadelphia, knows who some of them are?

If you believe him, then you have to go back with him to the year 1920, when he pulled a young man named Zret out of a deep hole into which he'd fallen and hurt himself.

Zret is a Venusian. And he told Coe an amazing story.

His ancestors came from a planet in our galaxy called Norca. They had to leave Norca

when it became dry. Some landed on Venus, others on Mars.

Eventually, they made their way to earth, on which they established five colonies some 13,000 years ago. One was on the lost continent of Atlantis. They left after atomic war broke out.

They repaired to Venus, where most of them live today in cool, mountainous regions of the planet.

Their research laboratories, says Albert Coe, their official spokesman, lie underground on Mars, and the Venusians shuttle between the two planets in their spaceships.

All but about 100 of them, that is, who live right here, on earth, some of whom Coe gets together with at least a dozen times a year.

Coe receives instructions by letter from Zret as to what he should tell the rest of the world. But he has none on hand to offer in the way of proof.

"I have strict instructions that as soon as I get a letter, I destroy it," he told MIDNIGHT. "I've never violated them."

Believed to be the only known photo and clipping about Albert Coe.

STARFALL
By ALBERT COE
CHAPTER 1
A CANOE TRIP AND
CHANCE MEETING

The story's initial setting is found in the eternal beauty of nature, in her forests and mountains, the blue skies above and on the tumbling streams that cut through a primal wilderness. It is June of 1920 and two teenagers, on vacation from school, had shipped their canoe and equipment to Canada and from there to follow the down river currents, back home to Hastings on Hudson.

We pick up the canoe, in lengthening shadows, as it silently glides over the surface of Trout Lake and introduce its two paddlers, my pal Rod and myself. We were heading for a shoreline banked with tall pines, silhouetted in black, against the brilliant hues of a setting sun. Here we pitched tent and after preparing supper, sat down to eat in the warming glow of our campfire, that held up the descending darkness and helped to dispel the few qualms that imagination finds in its presence. But the grandeur of this magnificent land, and whip-or-wills call in the twilight and the weird cry of the laughing loon on the lake at night, all seemed to blend into a song of adventure, that wove itself into the breathless anticipation of our start down the Mattawa River next morning. I never dreamed that an incident, not even remotely connected to the theme of this venture, was to take place and that it would definitely influence all my thought trends, in fact, to mold part of my

1

life in all the years that were to follow.

For the next three days we made our leisurely way downstream, camping, fishing, exploring; the excitement of shooting the rapids and carrying our canoe around a couple of jams caused by uprooted trees, logs and debris. At one jam we had to hoist our canoe over a rocky escarpement with ropes to get to clear water on the other side. At the third one of these barriers the river branched into several small streams, ponds and swamp. Being late afternoon we decided to camp for the night and await morning to find an easy way through and locate the main channel of the river at the other end.

We were up at the crack of dawn, caught and cooked two pickerel. After breakfast we watered down the fire and started out on foot to find an accessible passage through or around this tangled morass. My pal took the right side, I went left and had traveled about a half mile, over extremely rough terrain that posed an impossible portage. My curiosity getting the better of me as to what lay ahead kept me going and as I was clambering up the side of an out cropping of rocks, near the top I heard a muffled cry for help. I looked around, but could see no one, for it was thickly overgrown with small trees and bushes, so I climbed up over the edge and let out a yell.

Slightly to the right and ahead of me came an answer. "Oh help, help me. Down here." I still couldn't see anyone and had walked about twenty- five feet in the direction of the voice when I came to a five foot wide cleft in the base rock that ran diagonally toward the river. Wedged down in this narrowing crevice was a young man with his head some two and a half feet from the surface. He only had one arm free, so I reached over and grabbed his wrist but could not budge him. I cut down a tall sapling to use as a lever, and working my rope under the pit of his pinned arm, circled it around his back and chest, bringing a loop to ground level at the same time telling him I would try to pry him out. If I failed, I told him not to worry, for my pal was somewhere on the other side of the river and between the two of us we would free him.

Slipping the pole through the loop and using the opposite edge as a fulcrum point, I gave a heave and felt him move. Raising the lever end higher I propped it on a tree branch, jumped the crevice and pulled him out. His legs were so numb, that he could not stand and the left hip, knee and shin were badly lacerated. He first asked for water so I scrambled down the rocks to the river and utilizing my old felt hat as a bucket, relieved his thirst. Slitting a couple of my bandanas, I bathed the wounds and bound up his knee, shin and ankle, for they had started to bleed again. Under a rip in his suit, I placed a cold damp cloth for a pack on his hip.

As I was helping him my curiosity was rising as to the identity of my "patient." I told him of our trip and that I had been searching for a way to open water, at the same time noticing he was wearing an odd silver gray, tight jumper type garment that had a sheen of silk to it. It had a leathery feeling without a belt or visible fasteners attached, but just under the chest was a small instrument panel. Several of the knobs and dials were broken, from being jammed against the rock in his fall. Being so many miles from any form of civilization, I pointedly asked where he was from, if he was on a canoe trip, also when and what had happened to cause his misfortune.

He said that he was not canoeing, but had a plane parked in a clearing, three or four hundred yards down stream and had started out early the previous morning to do some fishing. In attempting to jump over the crevice, the loose earth and moss had given way underfoot and he had just about given up all thought of ever getting out alive when he heard some of the stones, loosened in my ascent, bouncing down the rock. Although not certain whether it was man, animal or just a small slide, he decided to cry out and said that my answering yell was like a miracle, for even though he had hoped, did not actually expect to hear a human voice in this deep wilderness.

He asked for my name and address and told me that he also lived in the United States and would surely write, as he would be eternally grateful, for giving him back his life. He was carrying a small tackle box and a fishing rod when he fell and asked if 1 would look for them. I searched and couldn't locate the tackle box. It had probably fallen into the crevice, but I did find the fishing rod under some brambles and the mystery of this strange person deepened within me.

The peculiar outfit, a plane landing in this rocky forest and now a fishing rod, the likes of which I had never seen. The butt was about three quarters of an inch in diameter and had the same leathery touch as his suit, but bright blue and formed a slight rounded protuberance just above it. It had a tiny slot in either side and continuance in a slender aluminum like shaft. It had no guides or reel, for the line came directly out from the inside at its tip, as a fine filament, to which was attached a conventional dry fly. I asked where he had purchased such a rod and the question was partially parried with a reply that his father was a research engineer and it was one of his own design.

The circulation had returned to his numbed limbs and although I noticed a few grimaces of pain, tended to ignore it. His overall composure as extraordinarily calm without apparent reaction to stress or shock, which usually would be evident after such a long and torturous ordeal, but I did suggest a helping hand back to his plane.

The offer was declined. He said, by his observation from the air, that my pal and I had five to six tough miles ahead of us. The opposite side, to him, looked lower, far less rocky and thought perhaps we could pull the canoe through some of the shallow, swampy water, dragging it over many of the lesser obstacles. He did not want to impose on me any further and said I had better think of starting back, for he had already been quite a burden.

From the condition of his leg I doubted that he could even walk, but made no comment, as I helped him up. He took two steps, swayed and grabbed a tree to keep from going down. I threw one arm around his waist, lifted his left arm over my shoulder and insisted that he again accept my aid, if for no other reason than just plain human compassion. 1 just couldn't let him go off alone, for if he fell and broke his neck, my time surely would have been wasted. He finally gave in, but on the condition of a promise; asking for my solemn word that I would not divulge to anyone, not even my partner, anything that had taken place today, or what I may see.

He then told me that his father had developed a new type plane that was still in an experimental stage and highly secret, but he often helped in the lab when home from school. As sort of a test, his father, had permitted him to use the plane for this fishing trip. In the future he would fully explain the reason for his request that I keep my promise. I agreed, so after half supporting and carrying him over some of the real rough spots, we finally made our way to a small clearing. Not more than seventy or eighty feet wide and near its center stood his "plane." I had been trying to figure how to get a plane in or out of here, without hitting a tree or protruding rocks.

What secret gimmick could launch one without a runway? I had fully expected to see some type of conventional aircraft and the reason for the reluctance in my accompanying him became crystal clear, for what I was looking at astounded me! A round silver disc, about twenty feet in diameter was standing on three legs in the form of a tripod, without propeller, engine, wings or fuselage. As we approached, I noticed a number of small slots around the rim and it sloped up to a rounded central dome. I had to duck to walk with him underneath, between the legs, although it was slightly concave and only about four and a half feet from the ground. He said, "Surprised?"

That wasn't actually the word for it, but I did not press him with questions, realizing he was suffering a great deal of pain. He reached into the end of one of three recessed in its bottom that fanned center wise from the base of each leg, pressed a button and a door swung down with two ladder rungs molded on its inner surface. I clasped my hands under his good foot and boosted him in. He peered down at me, over the rim of the opening and said, "I will never forget you for this day. Remember to keep your promise and stand clear when I take off."

I retraced my steps to just within the trees at the side of the clearing and turned to watch. I was musing over its lack of windows or port holes and wondered how he could see out, unless they were on the other side. Just then, the perimeter edge began to revolve. At first it gave off a low whirling sound, picked up speed mounting to a high pitched whine, finally going above the audible capabilities of the ear. At that time 1 experienced a throbbing sensation, which was felt rather than heard. It seemed to compress me within myself. As it lifted a few feet above the ground, it paused with a slight fluttering, the legs folded into the recesses as it swiftly rose with the effortless ease of thistledown, caught in an up draft of air and was gone.

I started toward camp, a little bewildered, for it all

seemed like a pantomime of unrealities. It was an episode lasting not much more than an hour that may have carried me a thousand years into the future and yet left an uneasy feeling of witnessing something that did not actually exist, an impression of disconnected sequences only found in dreams. A mere youth entrusted with such a wonderful invention, the peculiar suit, the odd fishing rod, the jagged rock of the crevice and began to wonder if it were not I, who had fallen, knocked myself out and was suffering the distortion of a stunned brain. I ran back to hunt for the tackle box, without success, but part of a blood stained bandana, the lever pole, its stump and branches were still there.

I arrived in camp first, kindled a small fire and put the left over coffee on to heat, but my thoughts were dogged by the strange sequel of events that my mind kept reliving step by step. Although I could not fasten onto a logical explanation that I had seen and touched a solid metal object, without even the rudimentary elements that have always been associated with flight, whether natural or invented by man. Even a balloon had to be filled with gas before it would go up. I had also watched this object whisk away like a flying carpet under a sorcerer's magical spell.

The coffee pot boiled over snapping me out of my thought trance, and I was pouring a cup when Rod returned with information that he had travelled a couple of miles, more than half of it being low, marshy and a lot of debris partially submerged.

He figured, by attaching our ropes to the bow ring we could drag the canoe through most of it. Even though I could hear Rod's voice explaining, my thoughts wandered back to my newly acquired, strange friend, what he had said about the surrounding area. It coincided with what Rod was now telling me. I knew then, that all l had experienced was very real and made a silent vow, never to break my promise unless released from it. My new friend was rapidly assuming the romantic status, in a young impressionable mind, of a good luck genie or wood sprite who had really come to test me.

The side I had explored was nothing but rocks and outcroppings. We finished our coffee, and as the day was turning quite warm, stripped down to bear necessities, including our moccasins and the ritual bandana with hat pulled down over it. We rigged the guide lines on the canoe and started our long trek toward open water. The rest of the day proved comparatively uneventful. With a little hard work, here and there, we cleared the last of the obstacles before the sun went down and camped on the bank of a now widening river, within ear shot of the distant muted whispers of a rapid's roar.

Morning dawned fair and lovely, as we waded downstream, to fish the quickening riffles above the head of the rapid and soon landed four nice trout. After an enjoyable breakfast, we pushed out into the river, eager to pick up the challenge of the rapid ahead and although quite swift, did not present too much difficulty. But, only an exhilaration in the test of skill, did we fight to keep our canoe from swamping, turning broadside to the flow or piling up on the many rocks that broke the surface. The rapid had tapered off to a fast run requiring only an occasional dip of the paddle for guidance. We completely relaxed in the ethereal enchantment of its beauty, gliding as silently down river as its own now quiet current cutting through a breathtaking panorama of valley and mountain. I glimpsed the blue sky above and beyond, wondering what part of this vast expanse my "stranger" and his unique flying machine, really called their own.

What tremendous force had the mind of man conceived to counteract the power of gravity on a solid metal object? Was its limitation to travel as boundless as the stars? I looked up at the sun and at the graceful trees reaching their slender fingers towards its warmth and light. For some unknown reason the peculiar phrase, "Man is master of all that he surveys," flashed across my mind. Yet, the instant of its passage jangled a discordant note. Probably a thousand years ago two Indians in a birch bark canoe floated over this very spot, looking in a pride of possession through their power. To them the awe of its grandeur may have even become an inclusion to a dream picture of a "Happy Hunting Ground" with its "Great Spirit," in an unknown beyond.

But now they are gone, and a million years before them a mighty Mastodon stood on yonder rock ledge, surveying his domain, as its undisputed "master," but he also is gone. In the dim mists of a hundred million years the gigantic Dinosaur could not have been denied this thought, but he too is gone. Musing a million years hence, what new form of "transient" will Nature then watch stake a fleeting claim here, to bask in his moment of glory under the majestic serenity of her eternal reign? Truly, as you gaze around from the smallness of a tiny canoe seat, the contemplation of her far reaching and overpowering greatness, dwarfs the thought of mastery to insignificance, as man himself becomes lost in the magnitude of her limitless creations.

With each passing day our journey assumed a more story like status, like dreams coming true, that stretched back into the imaginative yearnings of early childhood. Reminiscing of little side trips into unexplored streams, a trek up the mountain side to a hidden lake, the deer of early morning at the rivers edge, an occasional moose nibbling the bottom vegetation of a quiet cove and to me, an underlying intrigue in the mystery of my secret. Many times I would glance up, hoping to glimpse a flash of silver and that was my last impression, as he disappeared into the blue.

Juncture was made with the Ottawa River and during the next two weeks we became lost in a magical world of nature's caprices. Her whimsical moods changing from the chaos of dismal portage around a log jam, in a drizzle of rain, to the wonder of a scenic splendor. Then untamed power, as a quiet flow suddenly transformed into churning, thundering, foam flecked water of a rapid, only to again soften in the unearthly beauty of pictures painted by the sun, as it descends into darkness, but each one leaves its separate imprint that could never fade from the heart.

We were camped for the night, less than a days paddle from the city of Ottawa. Supper was over, the utensils washed and Rod had the lamp in the tent writing a letter to his girl, which he intended to mail when we reached the city. It was such a beautiful night that I decided to stay outside for awhile. So I stretched out, head resting on a blanket over a log and my feet toward the glowing embers of the campfire, to relax, in a contentment found in the curling smoke of a pipeful of tobacco and a setting that would never lose its closeness to my heart. The solitude of the vast forest seemed to drop away with the sigh of the wind whispering through the needles of her pines, the hum of insect lift was on the air, the bright chirp of the cricket and an occasional basso "ga-rump" of a bullfrog, blending with the soft lap of the rivers water flowing by the earth of its boundary.

All this composed a wordless song that welled deep from within nature's own soul. The sky was crystal clear with its millions of stars twinkling and dancing in their infinite dimension, but still an unfathomable, as mysterious as the night of man's first conscious perception of them. The intrigue of this mystery captured his mind as, in an eternal quest, he sought to reach out through the fantasy of imagination and bring them within scope of his intelligence or to endow with the beauty of divine inspiration that may intertwine spirit with body. Life seemed so full with the wonders of nature, without end, but as I half soliloquized, half pondered the thought, if, when I grew older and was burdened with the cares of responsibility, the concentration on occupational endeavor and the hustle bustle of modern daily tasks, would I too, in a year's span of time not even glance once at a star studded sky and would I lose this close affinity in all of God's creations, that I now feel so strongly, to a callous indifference? A tendency I noticed to be so prevalent in my elders.

My musing was interrupted as I caught a glint of silver over the tree darkened outline of the hills across the river, that disappeared for a few seconds and then I was sure, as it came straight toward me and the narrowing distance necessitated a raise in my line of vision and there, framed in a background of stars was my strange friend's stranger plane. He hovered motionless, not more than seventy feet above me and just off the shoreline. Then dipped from side to side in an unmistakable gesture of hello, through this simulated hand wave and continued on, to be lost from view over the forest behind me. I knew that it was his way of telling me that he was well again and I made a mental note, that if ever I did meet him, to surely question as to how he could know my exact location in the darkness of night. The tobacco had long since burned out in my pipe and after watering down the smoldering embers of the fire, crawled into my blankets, for my pal was sound asleep.

It was the last time that I was to see or hear from this

recondite pair, mysterious aircraft or personage for the next several months, although they did occupy a good deal of my thinking during the remainder of the journey. More than once I weighed the thought of taking Rod into my confidence, or to question, if he had seen the peculiar craft, but each time those last words, "remember to keep your promise," predominated and I kept silent. The entire course of travel with its highlights, uncertainties and the unending anticipation of what may lay around the next bend of a river, was so absorbing, that the summer just seemed to fly by, as we arrived home a week late for the new school term. We had lived many of the glorious adventures that most kids find only in the pleasure of reading.

It was a bit difficult to buckle down to the prosaic routine of scholastic endeavor, following so close to the end of this thrilling venture. Later events proved that it was not the end of a journey and my studies would continue many years into the future, for it was only the tiny thread that linked to a far greater voyage, through knowledge, to the infinite reaches of the universe. One that delved hundreds of millions of years in time, to the basic beginnings of a planet and its evolving life cycles and yet to span the incredible distances of the void, to another solar system of another race of beings.

The graphic story, which now unfolds, could not have been given life by me, if it were not for this unforgettable incident of my youth.

The Rescue

This illustration shows our usual attire in the early morning chill of the wilderness. Moccasins, long trousers, a flannel shirt and a bandana covering the forehead and draping down to the shoulders, with a felt hat pulled down over it. Our accessories always included a waterproof box of matches, sheathed hunting knife, belt axe and a coil of rope. The draped bandana and felt hat were to ward off the black flies that, at times, became quite an annoying problem in the deep wilderness. This garb of the forest is actually woven into a survival pattern, for man stands quite alone, when the adversity of nature overtakes him. In the progress of my stop, you will become aware of the separate roles these items played in a rescue and rudimental first aid that enabled the preservation of a life.

13

CHAPTER 2
AN INVITATION TO LUNCH

I had been home three months and it was almost six months since my initial encounter with the "stranger" and I was beginning to think that he had forgotten all about me, when on Tuesday in the second week of December, I received a letter signed "Xretsim" asking me to meet him in the lobby of the Hotel McAlpine, at 12:30, on the following Saturday and have lunch together. My heart skipped a few beats as I read and reread that letter. Saturday did not seem that it ever wanted to arrive, but when it finally did come I was all spruced up and ready to go by 8:30 in the morning, even though my train did not leave until 11:00. Mother remarked that I really must have an extra special date.

I did have a few "butterflies," wondering if I would remember his face. I entered the lobby as he came toward me with outstretched hand and the greeting of, "You surely look a lot different than when we first met," which echoed my own thought, doubting very much if I would have recognized him in the conventional suit, white shirt and tie. I first asked the pronunciation of his name and inquired about his injuries. With a mischievous chuckle he replied, "Just call me Zret for now. In the future you will figure it out. Thanks to your timely intervention with first aid, the leg and I are in good shape."

There were a million questions on the tip of my tongue,

14

as we were seated at our table, but most remained unuttered as he carried a good part of the conversation regarding trip, my school work, activities, ambition, etc. He told me that he had spot checked our progress, as far as Ottawa, to be sure we were O.K.

He cleared up the mystery of the night I saw his plane, explaining that he was fishing on the opposite bank, when we set up camp and could see my outline by the embers glow, as he stopped to wave hello.

After lunch he told me I would not hear from him for the next two or three months, but promised a fishing contest on the first nice Saturday of Spring. The general trend of conversation was a little disappointing, for I had wanted so much to know all about his little plane, where he lived and his activities. I realized he purposely avoided being led into any real information concerning himself, although I somehow sensed a very strong mutual bond between us. As he left he turned with a knowing look, saying, "In time all your unasked questions will be answered, for of all the men on this planet, you are my life. This salient fact is unforgettable." I did not think I had done anything so great until 1 later learned how close he was to the abyss of death, without a glimmer of hope, on that fateful day. 1 received a package, just before Christmas, containing a beautiful flyrod, reel, line and an assortment of flies and bass bugs, with a card. It was not until the later part of April that a note came to meet him in the Railroad Station at 5:00 A.M. on Saturday, for the promised fishing expedition. I knew that it was a forlorn wish hoping that it would be a trip in his plane. But, like the fishing equipment he sent for Christmas, he met me in a regulation automobile as we headed for Lake Mahopac, on what turned out to be one of the memorable meetings of my life.

A Friendly Hello

The basis of this picturization will forever leave a touch of the unreal in my memory. Materializing like a ghost, from the darkness across the river, to glide slowly, noiselessly toward me; then hover motionless, just above and beyond the shoreline. Even though I knew what it was; knew that it was guided by a ,"human" hand, in dipping from side to side in friendly acknowledgment, a prickly sensation raced through my body. I could not dispel the impression of a supernatural entity, as it silently slipped above the trees and was lost in the darkness behind me.

CHAPTER 3
THE FISHING TRIP
AND OFFER OF
TEACHING

He questioned whether I had mentioned him to my parents, but my answer was no and never would. He was a very deep, cherished secret and this knowledge I had, would be guarded as though it were the map to a buried treasure. He laughed, "You really are a romanticist aren't you? Your blond hair, blue eyes, the feeling of compassion and the great sense of beauty that you find in nature are almost identical to my own features and character. They mark you as a true throwback to my ancient ancestors, who discovered these lands so long ago. You probably already have an inkling that I'm a stranger to your modern world. This decision of explanation is a personal responsibility. Our mission here will forever be cloaked in the tightest secrecy.

"If the events that we foresee do not come to pass, our presence will not become known. The great depth of gratitude that I feel toward you, coupled with the things that you have seen and know exist, has influenced a violation of an inhibited law of disclosure. I feel that the entire incident stemmed from the hand of fate, for my predicament of that day had only about one chance in fifty million of ever occurring and the probability of rescue from it, at an even higher mathematical figure. I am sure if you can be as tight lipped in the future, as you have been in the past, that I will have nothing to fear, but a breach of this

17

trust could result in the direst of consequences."

He also said, without any reflection on my integrity, to honor this trust. He preferred that his true identity here, his address and personal life remain his secret, but offered to teach the vast wonders of the universe in a lifelong friendship, one in which he could only be known as "Zret." These words of caution, kindness and a heart warming handclasp cemented a bond of the oddest association imaginable, yet one that has never been broken.

We stopped at a diner, outside Tarrytown, to have a bite of breakfast. While we were eating he remarked, "By the way, did you figure the name out?" It was quite by accident, but I had, for the Christmas card was sitting on my bureau and it had tipped over, with its face to the mirror and as I combed my hair, there in plain English was "mister X." I picked up the card and an implication I had not given a thought to, was plain to see. "Xretsim" was "mister X" spelled backwards. He asked how I had explained the gift for although it was an involuntary impulse of the heart, realized afterward that it was also a bit thoughtless. I told him, "Oh, that was easy, for it was credited to one of my girl friends in New York and that we had a secret code which was often used in correspondence."

During the remainder of the ride he discussed the events leading up to our first meeting and that he was only one of a group of men, who had come to observe our scientific advance. In earth reality he was a student majoring in electronics at school and at the time of our meeting was on summer vacation.

He had taken advantage of the vacation time period to rejoin some of his own people, who operated one of their established bases off the planet and in the personal utilization of the little craft, could enjoy the wonderful fishing of the otherwise inaccessible rivers and lakes of Canada.

On leaving the base he had told his buddies not to worry if they did not hear from him for a week, as long as the all clear tone signal emitted in its regular twenty minute equivocal time cycle, from the ship. He told me this was his first inexcusable mistake.

"For you to thoroughly understand the astronomical odds against my ever being in the untenable situation that you found me and why I feel so strongly that fate destined our meeting, I will have to describe a few of the higher electronic principles of an electrodynamic cell, that we call the human body and how, through a method of amplified frequency we have woven these stepped-up energy waves into the control panels of our craft. You probably remember the little panel that was attached to the front of my flying suit. Well, attached within the suit are a series of what I will simply term electrodes, that come in contact with various nerve centers of the body.

"At the back of my neck, under the base of my brain are two more, the left one receiving brain impulses and the right one receiving all signals from the pituitary gland, the "Master Switch' of the body. All these comparatively weak waves feed into a section of that panel below my chest and any impulse of stress or emergency thought should have been transposed and amplified through it, to automatically record in the craft's control and change the all clear signal to a rapid tonal wave of distress. Help would have arrived in three or four hours. The manual controls of this panel also activate many of the functional duties of the craft, even to an unmanned flight back to its base.

"This sketchy detail of the safety features incorporated in the design of all our ships and the absolute synchronization of these electronic devices with the pilot, through the frequency coordinator of the flying suits panel, should give you a fairly good idea of the impossible odds of an unrecorded accident. Although the little manual adjusting knobs themselves, may be subject to fracture under certain shock stress, the internal mechanism is indestructible or I should add, was thought to be, until this incident. This was the first operational failure we have ever experienced with this type control.

"Research investigation later revealed a freak of electronic vacuum had caused an energy rupture between power pack and coordinator rendering the entire system, deader than the rock against which it was jammed. I had no way of determining this true state of affairs and I struggled to free myself, being more concerned with the ribbing I would have to take from my buddies as the intrepid fisherman who had sallied forth and without wetting a fly, needed a rescue team to pull him out of a hole into which he had thoughtlessly blundered, for even a rank amateur should have tested the footing, prior to an attempted leap.

"But I was not long in discovering the hopelessness of self extraction, for I could not even free my right arm, as the wrist was too tightly pinned between the panels face and the rock surface, so I concentrated on the distress signal and tried to relax in this painful trap, until help arrived.

"I still had no adverse thought as to my ultimate rescue and-only hoped they would hurry, for the feeling was leaving my feet and legs and I did have some minor internal injury to the lower part of my stomach. When the sun slid past its zenith, I knew something was very wrong and tried desperately to wedge my fingers onto the manual controls, never once entertaining a notion of its complete failure. My greatest battle of that terribly long afternoon and night was to keep from slipping into unconsciousness, for I knew that one lapse would be the sleep from winch I would never awaken.

"In discussing mistakes, I must include a third, which was my refusal of your aid back to the ship, as I was really only half alive and still laboring under the delusion that I could dispatch my signals. It was only through your adamant stand and a genuine concern of my condition, that I finally gave in and have often shuddered at the thought of what my fate would have been if you had nonchalantly taken me at my word and left. Another thing I will never fully determine is how you accomplished the Herculean task of carrying me up the side of that rocky ravine.

"When you put your shoulder under my stomach to lift me I passed out for a few seconds, probably as inert as a sack of wheat draped over it, until consciousness returned with that jolt, when you sat me down at the top, to help me to my feet and those last agonizing steps to the ship. Once inside, the shock of truth was a forceful substantiation to my narrow margin of survival, with only you as the bridge, for its control panel was still transmitting the intermittent wave of surety.

"This, I immediately switched to emergency distress and it was not many minutes after setting the automatic "homing" device that I collapsed, to later learn I was 'picked up" by one our larger ships that had intercepted the distress call and taken me aboard, craft and all.

"Despite a method of therapy, through applied electronics to eliminate infection and speed the healing chemistries of the body, it was almost a week before I was well and on my feet again.

"Ever since that last little wave of good-by, when you ducked out from under the ship, my greatest wish was that you could keep your promise, for it was the absolute factor in determining whether it became a permanent gesture or only 'so long.' The silence of the intervening ten months, broken with just a brief personal visit at lunch and a Christmas gift was, in a sense, actually part of a test. Although some principles involved in this explanation may at present, be a bit beyond your complete understanding, the expression of gratitude is given with a deep feeling of felicity. If this chance meeting of fate had only resolved as a passing incident, it would have left a little void within me that time would be long in filling and as it wings, its everlasting flight onward, who can foretell the far reaching contingencies this symbol of trust may invoke, perhaps if we stretch our thoughts, even to the stimulus that may reforge a broken link between past and present.

"My persistence with our ruling council was as dogged as the kindly determination that had made me accept a helping hand and they realized, only too well, that without this aid I could never have stood before them to plead your case. When tentative acceptance of you was finally approved and a leniency of certain explanation and teaching granted, I felt more strongly than ever that some strange power destined this one plenary course. Now that this little speech is off my chest, let's forget there are any worlds between us and as true pals, enjoy our days fishing with the only questions or worry as to the big one that got away and I'll 'betcha' a cup of coffee I catch the biggest fish."

We arrived at the lake and had been casting along the shore for a few hours, with fair success, when we came to a log with several turtles sunning themselves on its floating end and on our approach they all slid into the water. He paused and remarked, "you know, Al, those little fellows have been doing that same thing for millions of years and are one of the rare specie that have survived the countless evolutionary phases of your planet, in practically unchanged form and belong to a basic order of all animal life." Given this tiny opening, the hundreds of pent up questions that raced and tumbled in my head, spilled out like the bursting of a dam.

How old was he really? Where did he come from? Did he believe in God? Where is heaven? What makes his little ship fly? Was he married? Did he have children? Do they go to school? What kind of houses do you live in? He threw up his hands and said, "Whoa, you sound just like a babbling brook, but in all fairness I do owe you, at least, a rudimental insight to the unfamiliarities which will predominate your studies with me. We might as well start now, for it is time for a break and a bite of lunch, so let's pick a comfortable spot and during the next couple of hours, I will try to satisfy some of your curiosity.

"The things that you already know and this line of questioning, I am quite aware that my appearance does not belie the fact, in your mind, that I am considerably older and although the functional ability of my body, through our revitalizing methods, is actually not much more advanced in ageing processes than your own. The tremendous difference of age is going to startle you. In earth's time standard I am exactly three hundred and four years older than you. This reversal to youth was a vital requirement in establishing our identity as earthlings, for the foundation block in the fulfillment of our mission here, depended upon being accepted by your various races, as their own.

"Our home is quite simple to explain and is actually two worlds, one the planet Mars, nearing the end of an evolutionary life and the other, planet Venus younger in evolutionary processes than Earth, but its higher regions are not too drastically different than the environment here. The long and intricate details will have to await future discussion."

The direct answer to his incredible age and dwelling

on two planets was a shocker that left me speechless and I might add, a little apprehensive for a few minutes, but before he could skip on to another question, I regained my tongue and interrupted with, "It may be very simple to you, but why do you live on two worlds and come to still a third, our planet, as a boy?" He thought a moment and replied, "A very logical query and it is good, for as we talk it recalls to mind, another place, another teacher, another pupil, Greece, Plato and Aristotle.

"They often chose the solace of a setting, as we do now, under the trees and sky to conduct their debates and I mention this for it concerns a miracle of evolutionary refinement, the 'Brain.' It was the powerful, if not fully matured brain of Aristotle that contributed a lasting influence on the cosmology, which is embodied in your next two questions, just as the immaturity of a composite 'Brain' destined a man very old in years, but of a more highly evolved mental attitude, to masquerade as a youth of your own race.

"To start off, you must realize that one question and answer will inevitably pave the way to hundreds of others, so you must also learn to practice a little patience, for it is impossible to cram the result of thousands of years of research and history into a few brief hours. But, as your studies advance, question and answer will become the integral breath in every step, as you reach for a complete understanding. This first lesson of elementals, confined to some of your questioning, will then of necessity be broached in generalities, which I want you to ponder.

"You will find your initial impressions will be underlined with the confusion of comparisons, contradictions, and dissident tenets, in their confliction with accepted tradition and the established routine of study in your own educational systems. I do hope that you will continue to pursue your education with all diligence, but you will find, as we break down the composite components of natural law and documented history, the analysis of your brain will formulate opinion and that this analogy will definitely bear on all of your future thinking. This gift of a more complete knowledge, I give from my heart and somehow I know that it will not be abused, but only to enhance the joy and the beauty that you now find in nature's own priceless gift of life.

"Any question?"

My reply was in a rather negative vein, for the enormity of implication would have to sink in, but the aspect was still a little frightening for would I be the only one in the whole world to know these things? His kindly boyish smile was somewhat reassuring and he said, "Perhaps at present, they may not know all, but whoever can foresee the unpredictable in the trend of future events and knowledge, tempered with wisdom, should never foster fear.

"To give a little clarity to your puzzle of my 'complex' home and present residence on earth, I will cite an example of fact, with which you are familiar and lead from it to the core of your mystery.

"Only recently, many of the more 'intelligent' and 'cultural' nations of earth have concluded a long, bloody war and during its progress several innovations, designed in specifics to the mass slaughter of humanity were introduced such as, unproved explosives, war planes, Zeppelins, aerial bombs, U Boats, tanks and poison gas. In your scholastic studies of history, you have probably recognized the advance in refinement of weaponry over the centuries, as copper and bronze replaced the stone tipped arrow and axe. The steel lance and sword along with the crossbow, catapults, the horse and war chariots made those of bronze obsolete.

"Then gunpowder, rifles, cannon, chemistry and the latest mechanized media of delivery in this sudden, if untimely death, on land, sea and air. As each new discovery, new invention was applied to a military potential, its horizon broadened to the eventual horror, brutality and devastation that emerged as a 'World War.' This conversion of inventive genius from the brain of earth's inhabitants, to ever greater devices of destruction was the prime factor that motivated our mission, as we contrive to study and later on will ultimately work in the various professions to enable a determination of escalation, if, or when it continues to be the goal of an awakening field of science.

"Should a suspicion cross your mind that we may be spies, planning conquest of your lands, please dispel it, for your common sense should tell you, that if this were the case, I surely would not sit and discuss its details with you. As our association becomes closer, you will be convinced of this sincerity and that the pursuit of aggression, of subjugation and its accompanying brutality find no place in our philosophy.

"Now I will try to tie together the significance of Mars, Venus and Earth as segments concerned in your question. Each one holds its own traditional niche in—shall I say— the recent history of our race as it sought refuge from their own dying world of a slightly older sun and dehydrated planets.

"Mars is actually the ancestral stepping stone that some fourteen thousand years ago, gave the chance of life, to a pitiful few, that survived this transmigration of solar systems and will always hold a spot of deep affection in our hearts. If it were not for this unique little planet, an entire race of beings would have perished and lost its place in this scheme of things forever, a spark of life returned to the oblivion of its energy source.

"I will deviate for a few moments to talk of unusual elements in the Universe, undoubtedly an indefinable attribute of our creator, the Atom. This completely mystifies the brain and also defies the research of instrumentation, but at times directly influences the shaping of certain events and destinies.

"I mention this for they will often crop up in our discussions and will now isolate just one of these strange interveners that is simply termed in your language as 'Luck,' with its two sides of good or bad. This emphasis is on the good for it not only played an unmistakable role in the conclusion of this epic flight, by favoring one solitary ship, but was also quite evident in our meeting. In each instance, I know that without this presence, I surely would not be here to speak of it. Originally we even tried to connect it, in part, to a similar theory of your supreme being, but is far more intricate in scope, more subtle and is somehow wrapped up in the ceaseless and universal conflict of the opposites, cold, heat, negative, positive, etc. The method and motivation of its random appearance is the 'bugaboo' that our research has, as yet, been unable to define.

"So that we do not get in too deeply today, I will merely illustrate by our meeting. I was trapped and helpless, with every safety device our science had advanced at my fingertips, in fact even part of my body, and yet I felt my life was gradually slipping away, but with all the odds against me, there still was hope. With all adversity present, in the initial misstep and subsequent predicament, I will not detail, but only imply as the negative. Supposing that our places had been reversed that day, probably in effect, your first thought would have been, 'Golly I was lucky,' that he happened along and in these few words lie the crux of this analysis.

"Have you ever given any serious thought, as to why,

these peculiar events do or should happen?"

I said, "Not actually, but had often wondered about some incidents, particularly one of last whiter. Three of my buddies and I were hunting with twenty-two rifles and as I tripped over a root or something, falling forward, a bullet fired by one of the boys ahead, in a hasty 'pot shot' at a squirrel running up a tree, nicked my scalp. It turned out to be scarcely more than a scratch, that bled a bit, but if I had been walking upright it would have caught me in the chest and who knows? It still seems that some irresistible power pushed me down under that bullet and this we often consider, in the light of a miracle. I have also thought on several occasions, about the morning that we met. I almost turned back a couple of times, because the likelihood of lugging a canoe and equipment over that rugged terrain was pretty remote, but the curiosity of what may be ahead kept me going. Could this curiosity be connected?"

"Yes," he rejoined. "That is exactly what 1 mean, plus the controversial possibilities. One, the time element. If it had been later in the day or next morning, it would have been all over for me. Two, under the circumstances, your common sense told you to turn back, but you kept on. Three, you might have picked your way over the logs and debris at the foot of that rock point. Four, you could have moved further inland, where the rise was not quite so steep. Now the question with these possible alternatives, and the fact that it was a tremendously large wilderness, what intangible force directed your footsteps as you scrambled up that rocky knoll, the rubble loosening in the ascent, acting as a herald to your approach, to my almost exact location?

"This is the type of unfamiliarities that I previously mentioned. Some, like this one, we have not completely solved, but research has wrested their secrets from thousands of others and these 'whys' and 'wherefores' will constitute the bulk of your studies.

"To continue our discussion of Mars. This same element of 'Luck,' so to speak, took over an uncontrollable ship. Through an exact angle of tangent, enabled it to land with two thirds of its complement, still alive, on the only planet in the entire solar system that would not have destroyed her in atmospheric friction, chemicals or semisolid state.

"These hardy ancestors of mine then faced and overcame the planet's challenge of environment. Succeeding generations, once again, advanced to the scientific potential of launching twin probes, to Venus and Earth, both of which were subsequently colonized.

"In the primary stages of this expansion, bases of research were established on Venus to study her peculiar atmosphere, the geological composition and life complexes, as the main colonization was concentrated on Earth, where they encountered several races of primitive, but true human being. Here lies one of their great mistakes. Not withstanding a broad and comprehensive knowledge, they were in a sense, 'naive.' They were confronted with certain trends and conditions they had never before known or visualized. The deadly conflict of man unto man, an act of brutality to one another or to animals, and the jealousy of possession that was so apparent in these primitive men was actually shrugged off as traits; a phase that education would correct. So, they taught from five major centers that were founded during the next thirty years.

"One hundred years of teaching wrought an amazing transition to these general areas of contact, as former tribes of quarreling natives attained the status of men of science. Not once in this period was serious thought given to the fact that Earth's branch of humanity evolved from their earlier animal and primate orders, more than a half million years later than our own entrance to this stage of advancing life and must therefore be an elemental brain, thousands of years away from a point of refinement that could submerge the dominant predatory characteristics of its animal beginnings. The possible consequence evaluated, in view of this fact, that only time refines.

"Too late the realization dawned that the boon of intelligence only trained the mind and spread, like a thin veneer, over this natural basic instinct and when it surged to the fore, this fragile shell soon burst, as the tremendous power of knowledge that had been endowed with kindness and love, for the benefit of all, was debased to the greed of selfish possession and a product of science, harnessed with an urge to kill, that first introduced the horrible weapons of slaughter which could only be conceived through animalistic impulse and perfected by the intellect but immaturity of a human brain. When this device was used to conquer, it broke away from human control and the ensuing cataclysm exterminated a good deal of all life on Earth and our race was again shattered and broken.

"On Venus, the man form had not appeared and what was left of our people discovered that it was far more advantageous to weld the primal forces of nature into compatible existence, than the devious manipulation of an unruly brain, trained in intelligence, long before it had the ability to acquire the wisdom of equalizing culture, that gave predominance to love and compassion in a brotherhood of man.

"Today our basic home is the high land of Venus; although a good part of our research is still conducted on Mars, especially electronic probe, for its thin atmosphere and peculiarity of magnetic fields lends itself, as an ideal laboratory, to almost distortion free reception.

"The races of Earth we have left strictly on their own, having no desire whatever of repeating a mistake made by our ancestors; but in the probe of distant star systems, we have observed that an occasional explosion of a strategically placed planet, will completely destroy every other planet of a specific solar system and the debris reclaimed by its sun, which in some instances has also reacted in violent upheaval. The potential of planetary catastrophe has not yet been achieved by your war lords, in their headlong race to recreate the ultimate in destructive energies; but you may live to see the day of this probability.

"So we dwell among the various nations of people; just as you, family boys in our present role of students, unassuming and without thought of conquest, subversion or even interference in your way of life, but only to study trends. We are fully aware of the awesome power of a human brain and also that the pressure of animalistic ferocity, when released in the blind, unreasoning fury of battle, can strip away even its counterbalance of common sense. Should our concern materialize, we will not be caught napping this time, for our position here will enable the evaluation of suitable counteractive which, at least, would insure the status quo balance of planetary orbit."

I was becoming spellbound and lost in personal visualization as I tired to follow and comprehend his descriptions, although some were way over my head, as he spoke of planet and star systems, with the same assured familiarity, that I would mention a local train ride from Hastings to New York and his hint of releasing explosives that would, in essence, place the destruction of Pompeii, by Vesuvius, in the same category as a battle between two Indian war parties, was a bit hard to picture; but it did tie in with the fabled disappearance of Atlantis and I was content only to listen, rapt in admiration of his unusual knowledge. And he continued. . .

"The next two questions; Do I believe in God? Where is Heaven? are far more difficult to answer and queries that I could slough off in an affirmative vein, as both are based on half truths; but my promise of complete knowledge, extends to the limit of our advance in research and although my explanation probably cannot or will not be accepted by you, it is one that I must resolve as a scientist. The inspiration roots of this theology are buried deep in an actuality of appearance and teaching of my predecessors here so very long ago, but the evolvement of a supreme being and eternal life is a twisted version of natural phenomenon, distorted by vanity of ego and a greed for power. You and I were born under vastly divergent philosophies and as they have little or no parallel, will necessitate a sketchy outline and brief history of both. Ours a simplicity in the beauty of life, and yours a complex of compounded theoretical ideologies, which seeks to combine the joy of conscious realization and oblivion into rational doctrine that embraces a theory of etherial beauty in an everlasting land of plenty—though the estate of Death— truly a paradox.

"The basics, in our philosophies, glorify the supremacy of Being as, throughout our lives, we strive to enhance this joy of existence in an unselfish realm of love, that combines the benefit of science in a composite of mind and deed. This beauty of thought not only embraces the brotherhood of man but widens to encompass all matter manifestation, for we also emerge from this same tiny segment of an indeterminate whole and even though it gives an impression of unlimited boundaries, merely represents a minor pattern of this universal force; but each with its inalienable right to fulfill a fleeting design in a status of life. If a superior intellect can aid in the lot of those in lesser station, so be it; but if these entities reject or cannot benefit from an act of benevolence, they are left to pursue their own destinies, free and unmolested.

"Electronic survey of cosmic dimension discloses a magnitude of thousands of millions of light years, composing a chaotic cauldron of uncontrolled energy, in unceasing, restless motion and all the galaxies, graduating to the suns and planets, with their compliment of inorganic and organic bodies, comprise less than one percent of this energy mass. The formation of matter, at best, is merely a random association in the attraction of energy opposites, whose building molecules, create the unstable structures that we recognize in the objective. But energy and matter are in a constant state of interchange and this endless transition of one into the other identifies the phases, in your terminology of Life and Death.

"Life spans are as varied, as the untold millions of forms, that have been represented in this category. Some microscopic bodies complete a full cycle in a few seconds; the Mayfly: simulated in the dry fly that we used in our fishing today, matures, courts, mates, reproduces and returns to this oblivion of disconnected elements, in a day. You are probably familiar with the differing ages that insects, birds, animals, turtles, etc., achieve as we go upwards to billions of years for planets and suns.

"But, through chemical decomposition, erosion by friction or failure in a body's electronic fields to assimilate this energy of animation, all inevitably revert to the gases of constitution and many of these gases are reconstituted, perhaps not in previous pattern, but in some station of matter. In this primal law of negative, positive and interchange you will find the seed from which man of earth has invented his illusions of supernatural beings and of spirits dwelling in a paradise of eternal life; through a god's love and compassion if positive, or condemned to the tortures of a negative hell.

"As science further breaks down theory into relative components of truth, we are confronted with a irrefutable fact of "Creation" that places the premise of a discerning God creating a cosmos and dispensing His gift of life in a rather dubious light, for in this vast conglomerate of energy and matter there is one glaring deficiency. This elusive property is the emotion known as "Love and Compassion" and probing of many thousands of years which stretches back, far, far beyond, my predecessor's emigration from their own solar system, can only pinpoint this emotion and its characteristic of action, in the one infinitesimal composite element, defined as the "Brain." It reaches a certain predominance in the human brain and is present, though in minor station, in the brain of all lesser animals.

"To simply explain this ancient quest of its origin, a deep probe into the atom was instituted, that eventually uncovered the secret in the attraction of atom to atom. In the motivation of this coalescence, a great eagerness is displayed in a system a higher energy content to give up part of this energy to a system of lower energy value and although it only resolves as a geometric equation of physics, containing a minute spark of intelligence without emotion; but in this act of interchange a merging was discovered, not only the initial impetus that requires billions of years in evolutional refinement to raise to the cultural essence now present in the brain of your races and mine, but also the very root which creates the impelling desire of male and female to mate, in all plant and animal orders.

34

"A moot question of research arises regarding the type of organic life and its mental capacities, in the various solar systems, whose suns differ from our own and many peculiarities are noted. We have recorded electronic vibrations and frequencies which establish the fact, beyond any reasonable doubt, that on the planets of a number of these suns, life materialization does exist, but in structures composing compounds, other than those from which our life cycles stem, although determination of form, etc., cannot be established.

"Fixed structural codes are not an indelible stamp of universal order, nor are they interrelated from solar system to solar system, except in a compound procedure of evolutionary formula and these adaptations generally confined to a specific solar systems boundaries. The conformation of its myriad life complexes dependent on type of sun, its position in the galaxy and the galaxies perimeter location, in relation to the nucleus as it spins in its 223 odd million year cycle of rotation.

"This revolution of the galaxy may be compared to the earth's twenty-four hour rotation in relation to the sun, but each hour of earth's time standard would span several millions of years in the galaxy's time table. And, just as on earth, conditions change in the progress of this motion, but in far greater scope than the alternating light and darkness, temperature and climatic fluctuations that become part of an ordinary earth day, representing its one rotation, in relation to the sun.

"Even the violence of an occasional earthquake, volcanic eruption, blizzard or hurricane that appear in isolated instances, are as a summer zephyr to a tornado when comparing the awesome compulsions that the nucleus exerts on the planets of all solar systems in various stages and positioning of one galactic revolution. During certain phases it wrinkles a planet's surface to draw up tremendous mountain ranges or allows them to erode into low rolling hills. It triggers one major and two minor glaciation periods and its uneven pressure of pulsating energy, teaming up in assimilation by a sun, influences drastic temperature oscillations, it interferes with normal storm tracks causing either over abundant rainfall or extended periods of drought and in some cases completely dehydrates a planet. In the past it has sucked the two outer planets from this solar system and was the prime mover in the fragmentation of a third. In fact, the very existence of a planet and its life cycles are dependent on the whimsical reflexes between Nucleus, Galaxy and its specific Sun.

"Under these ever shifting conditions develop the myriad cycles that appear on a planet as Life; through energy grouping into molecular structures that take root in a then harmonious environment. But as upheaval, temperature and water diversification nullify these optimum tolerances, many specie reach a point of extinction and the adversity, that causes the extinction of these orders, becomes an acceptable environment to newer cells that bud and embark on their paths to evolutionary refinement or to some previous orders with the ability to readapt, but generally this adjustment creates a marked change in structural form and characteristic.

"Outside the bacteriological and minute plant and animal complexes there are exceptions to this overall picture in the larger animal, as some very ancient direct line specie have defied the ravages of time and still persist in original form; but most are confined to water or spend a major part of their lives, in water.

"By far, the older of these living fossils is the curious little character that is often tossed up on the beach, as he grubs the bottom under tide waters for worms, etc., and commonly called the Horseshoe Crab. Actually he is not a crab but a venerable ancestor of the brandling Spider clan and reached his peak of evolvement, as he is today, more than two galactic revolutions ago. A half galactic revolution later, the Turtle appeared and; shortly after, the Crocodile and except for some structural adjustments on head, jaw and breathing apparatus, lives today in unchanged form.

"As we jump ahead another half revolution, we encounter the Shark and Plesiosaur, (the mysterious "sea serpent" of sailor's tales) and just beyond midway of this last galactic cycle, in the jungle of the prolific Dinosaur, the odd little Platypus, now found in Australia, evolved as one of the early forging links between reptile and mammal. This unreeling panorama of test, trial, error, discard and reform are as convolutions in a rotating Kaleidoscope of ever changing pattern, color and design, but the "Atom" inevitably strives to raise its newer manifestation above a preceding specie, in a refinement of form and brain, which has led to the afore mentioned peculiarities in solar systems; even patterns of compatible suns, for instance our two of basic carbon compounds are not identical for thousands of plant and animal orders that have gained predominance on your planet during the past 700 million years, never appeared on our original planet and vice versa, although many are similar.

"So that I do not leave your brain in an utter state of confusion, regarding the tremendous time spans in a galactic cycle that I have compared to 24 hours of earth, let us imagine a galactic clock, fashioned in exact conformity to one of earth, with identical numerals from 1 to 12 around its face, but for each sweep of the second hand around the dial of an earth clock, that denotes one minute, would comparatively, tick off 155,000 years on the galactic clock. To establish a medium of parallel we will assume that an earth day starts at 12 o'clock high noon, when a specific zone on its curvature, reaches an apex in relation to the sun, a fixed point and, of course, earth's rotation tends to create a descending arc of this spot instituting your P.M. until midnight and the ascending arc of A.M. to the point of beginning, completing a day.

"Now apply this same reference of high noon, etc., to our solar system as its position in the galaxy reaches this same relationship to the universal nucleus, a similar fixed point, to start its new day. It is rather difficult to transpose our mathematics and calculus into spoken English, for several factors upset this apparent orderly progression and just as earth's tables of continuance vary and require adjustment over long stretches of time, there are fluctuations in galactic spin and orbital velocity as it often weaves a zig zag course due to pulsation of Nucleus energy flux that warps the magnetic line of force, in which it travels and also—in a true sense of the word—galaxies are not rigid entities; but, as a topic of evaluation, these figures and this principle will hold fairly accurate.

"However, we do base our tables of elapsed rotational times from these mathematically fixed entities; but, as a solar system in the galaxy approaches and passes this assumed point of high noon, the nucleus influence again pulls up the mountains and major glaciation periods or, as commonly known, great ice ages ensue on its planets and this point having been passed just over a million years ago, will bring our clocks into proportionate time perspective of 12.07 in a new galactic day.

"And in looking back, if we apply this same time value of our imaginary clock, we will see the elemental Homo Sapiens emerge from the primate genus at 10.20 o'clock and the last of the prolific Dinosaurs give up the ghost at 6 o'clock, to an intolerable temperature and climatic change of budding mountains and a minor glaciation period, as the solar system comes out from behind the bulk of the galaxy, between it and the Nucleus just as your position on earth comes out from behind the bulk of the planet, relative to the sun, at Dawn.

"I realize that I have thrown many curves at you today and do hope that you can grasp these fundamentals of physics, for it is an insight to the formulas on which our philosophies are based and the varied and random appearance of all things that are created, through the restless motion of universal force, is the underlying reason for these beliefs. We do not delude ourselves with any thought of permanence or extensions, after death as this transmigration of energy is momentarily fixed in the manifestation of matter; for even a billion years that may appear as an eternity to the human is a mere infinitesimal pause in this everlasting flight. With this truth in mind, we redouble our efforts to extend our limited span of Being and to it, endow all the wisdom, beauty, love and compassion that only a human brain may extol.

"And now, my friend, we have talked ourselves into the setting sun; so the time has arrived when we must terminate this delightful day, pack our gear and head for home, but can continue this discussion as we drive back."

While taking our rods apart, I mentioned that he had not used the little gem that I retrieved from the brambles, at our first meeting and he replied, nor am I wearing the flying suit, for those items belong to the other side of my life and like our identities cannot, at present, become part of your world. Also, in another truth, I would not take an unfair advantage in our fishing contest and by the way, that hot cup of coffee is going to taste doubly good, for the larger fish is in my catch, so you stand the treat. It seemed incomprehensible that anyone of such great age, could act as boyish as he, display the enthusiasm in little things, that most youngsters only enjoy, but his amazing trait was the unlimited source of knowledge, the easy manner in which he found expression and simple explanation of what I knew must be deeply involved mathematical problems, so that I may form a reasonable opinion of the strange and unfamiliar facets of our world.

(Mathematics did come easy to and Dad had given some pre-college tutoring in the complexities of engineering and architecture.)

Even his voice softened, as though with a tinge of regret in undermining the faith of ideals that I had believed in throughout my short lifetime; but in a directness that left no room for parry, no defense, against his logic and I had a very strong hunch that he could also prove his assertions. I doubt if I will ever forget that metal disc, with him inside, as it slowly ascended a few feet above ground and then in the twinkling of an eye, with only a flash of silver from a sun glint, it vanished. I realized it could not have evaporated and that he was not an apparition, for his handclasp was firm and warm, but a truth was slowly becoming apparent; that our educators had only a hazy inkling into this vast and mysterious universe.

No concrete knowledge to envision highly intelligent people dwelling on other stars, instead of angels, or the slightest conception of the inconceivable ships they used to traverse these tremendous distances. It was an awe inspiring thought to only conjecture that I may be permitted a tiny peep hole, to view some of its marvels. My feelings were actually difficult to determine as they ranged from walking on air to an uncertain puzzled boy, just a bit afraid of where it may all lead but did have a great trust in my "stranger," perhaps in the guise of hero worship and in his attitude toward me, could only find a correlation in the gentleness of a mother love, as she guides her baby through childhood.

Fascination, apprehension, fantasy, belief and doubt tumbled around in my head; mountains springing up and wealing down; Ice; Imaginative galactic clock; Turtles, Horseshoe Crabs, Crocodiles and Sea Serpents, like beads on an infinite string stretching into hundreds of millions of years. Energy, Gases, Objects, gases.

My thoughts were interrupted by his voice; quite silent aren't you? Are you deeply puzzled?

Overpowered, I replied, would fit better and you know every time I see one of those doggone turtles, pop off a log, I will picture a dim primeval swamp with all kinds of ooze and gases rising from its surface. He really laughed and said, so many of your impressions and perceptions have an unexpected uniqueness, all of their own and the unruffled composure, a knack of taking everything in stride, even to the first moment of our meeting, puzzle me at times, probably as much as I do you; but I am very sure that our comradeship will long endure in a most enjoyable vein, for your mind is sharp, and what is more, refreshing; it is an open mind. And now, with the same reluctance that you feel in terminating this day, we must leave and be on our way.

We had been riding for several .minutes, both lost in thought, when he reopened the conversation with an analysis of his views on our philosophies, by again retracing sequels through the corridors of time. As each incident fitted into its interlacing pattern, it seemed as though an intricate tapestry was being woven in pictures of unfolding history and the flow of his words carried me back to relive, step by step, every thought, fear and inspiration as a struggling brain sought an answer in this baffling but eternal quest of—Why?

"The glimmerings of present religious beliefs or philosophies, on your planet, stretch into its dim unrecorded mists of 10,000 years but did not become an obsession of the mind until about 8800 years ago, when an awaking racial remnant that had survived the self induced cataclysm of world upheaval, 4,000 years before, initiated the dawning of what is known as the early Eastern Cultures, as they partially revived the withered root of a former scientific knowledge; but its fragmentary principles were nurtured on greed, fear and a lack of complete understanding that eventually developed the mental hybrid which has given life to the millions of gods, totems, images and charms, that bridge these hundred of centuries.

"The myriad groupings of men, who have marched through these pages of time, each contributed an imaginative piece to fit into this mysterious puzzle of creation and the personification of energy, as god head, to which he endowed his own exclusive emotion of Love and its opposite, Severity as an attempt to control his environment, through a cajoling or appeasement of these fearful and incomprehensible forces of nature, in the supplication of prayer or ritual of sacrifice.

"Calamity; represented in earthquake, volcanic eruption, meteorites, thunder, lightning, flood and assorted disaster; an attribute to the wrath of a specifically designated god, through a participation in sin and adversity; prompting these sins against god, laid to influence of an evil spirit or demon that only the purification of religious reverence could erase. From this basic spirals the embellishment, as each creed, tribe or race created its own "True God" or complex of "True Gods" in an ever expanding divergency of thought and although they all worshipped the same true essence in the Deity, selfishness led to the narrow minded

42

chaos of intolerance and brutality, as each sect has fought to defend or impose on others, its own conception of this divinity.

"Christian doctrine combines several branchings from these earlier eastern cosmologies; notably; Magi, Egyptian, Babylonian and Hebrew, in a semi consolidation with findings of later Greek philosophers, in their diligent search for the primal stuff from which everything is made.

"Magi instituted the celestial paradise and transmigration of a good soul to its benefit of eternal life and the bad souls condemnation to the tortures of fiery demons. The Egyptian dramatized, in metaphysical sacredness, the transformation of one substance into another; seed into plant; the consuming of plant or animal by man, became man; malt and water changed to beer; dung materialized into beetles; chiseled and shaped stones into gods, etc. The body's loss of animation also released its soul, that started a hazardous journey to the judgement hall.

"After surviving many trials tribulations and purgatory, it faced a panel of questioning judges and the merit of this confession determined its fate. If true, the soul was presented to its god for his blessing and entered the land of everlasting plenty but a falsified confession condemned it to transformation into a black pig or the horrors of a devouring demon according to severity of infraction.

"Babylon donated the base belief of an orderly pattern in creation. Their exhaustive study, in the movement of heavenly bodies, revealed a regulated appearance of planets, stars and constellations that apparently controlled all the elements so essential to the livelihood of plant, animal and man. Characteristic, seasonal change, rainfall, drought, etc. (Also the base of modern Astrology). The Hebrew contributed God the Father and segments of its Torah.

The Greek philosopher sought his answers in abstractions rather than a true conformity to religious motivation and I will confine this analysis in a 200 year span, roughly from 600 B.C. as theory and debate finally resolved into an acceptable conclusion of Aristotle's logic. During this period many philosophers wrangled over the problem of a prime factor or factors and with the exception of one wedge of truth that was inserted, but discarded, will concentrate on the few that directly influenced the deductions of comparison that established the Aristotelian theory.

"As we enter this maze of mathematics and theoretical will-of-the-wisps we first encounter Pythagoras, scholar and mathematician, as he bends his efforts to confirm a belief that numbers are the ultimate elements of the universe and that his isolation of a quintessence, which he termed Aether, his supposed substance from which the heavenly bodies were composed, also represented the soul of man and death; the transmigration of this soul to its seat of origin.

"As we move deeper into this maze, a bedlam of voices reecho in argument and debate; one element, two elements, fire, three elements, ah, water are bandied back and forth until the voice of Empedocles rings out, loud and clear, expounding this theory that all things are made from a mixture of four basic elements; fire, water, air and earth. Proportionate fractions of each in the mix, determined whether bug, mouse, king, plant or mountain materialized.

"Our path widens considerably with the appearance of Leucippos and his pupil, Democritus, as they also questioned; what is matter? And in a completely new line of thinking; is it continuous? They tried to imagine chopping away at an object without ever reaching the final piece that could not be divided and as this posed an illogical mathematical equation, they concluded that matter must be discontinuous and that when the ultimate "atomon" (indivisible particle) was reached, it would vanish under the last chop.

"The further studies of Democritus convinced him that these invisible atomons, of varying shape and characteristic, were in a state of constant motion and the characteristic of each would either attract or repel one another, but; from those that did mate, were born the tiny building blocks that evolved into all the solids of matter. He did not have method or instrumentation to prove this theory and being so contradictory to all religious presumption of an orderly creation, by its gods, was subsequently denounced by them, under premise that if this hypothesis were true; the random attractions or repulsions of these atoms, as they flitted haphazardly about, could only create a disorganized universe without a vestige of moral purpose.

"So, the path narrows again into its unfathomable maze and the powerful brain of Aristotle, in creating his enduring shrine to the four elements, abetted by favor of the church, slammed shut the door on further research for well over a thousand years. As we glance around this colossal temple of the mind, our eyes fasten on its central pedestal, the irrefutable strength of syllogism and circling this symbol of deductive reasoning, stand its supporting pillars of common sense and the reflex to truth that observation in every day trends of life appear to sustain. It is a great pity that the brilliance of Aristotle's equative brain did not evaluate the intangibles in the theory of Democritus, rather than combine the tangibles of Empedocles with a distorted intangible of Pythagoras and, although it may be wishful thinking, may have advanced the philosophies in comprehensive doctrine two thousand years beyond their present station for the tenets resulting from this system of common sense were anchored on such solid ground that only the improving instrumentation of modern science has been able to shake one foundation stone of this massive structure.

"Its keystone of syllogistic logic may be illustrated by advancing relative statements that call for an answer to the specifics or original premise. For example: an initial assertion declares that all mammals are warm blooded; then adds: horses are mammals; which can only summarize in a common sense conclusion that horses are warm-blooded. In this line of reasoning. Aristotle's visual appraisal of the world seemed to bear out that its composition did embody a varied mixing of rudimental elements, as envisioned by Empedocles; but he deduced that specific properties were missing and to allow for tolerance of the myriad types in manifestation, added four qualities, two of each element.

"To the element fire, were added extreme heat and dryness; to air, lesser warmth and moisture: water, cold and wet; earth, cold and dry; thereby establishing a hypothesis that substance represents the various amounts of the four elements in the mixture and proportionate mixing of the four qualities, produced characteristic formation of every objective solid or conceivable intangible of the universe. To the mixture, in creation of a human, Aristotle concluded with an addition of the quintessence; Aether, the purest of the pure, as isolated by Pythagoras which not only confirmed man's noble station; just below the Angels, but above and with complete domination over all lesser entities.

This persistent surmise of being molded from a very special clay has given rise to a greatly inflated ego as man of earth assumed that he, this noblest of all the mortals, could only dwell on an equally exalted mortal station, as core or center of the universe, around which every other motivation revolved. In compressing the vast reaches of the universe, its great "God" of creative energy and his infinite billions of suns and galaxies into this equative ratio of a minute, stationary piece of real estate, in family community, he also compressed his mind in proportionate guise of community activity. Emperor ruled an empire, the general his army, a husband his household and even the child, its toy; so in this compact principle of pattern was formulated the dogma to personalize a private god, to guide or rule in overall jurisdiction.

"In concluding this brief analysis of basic segments that underline the myriad cults and their assortment of representative gods, only in the teachings of Christ can we determine an essence of the true universal God. A far reaching vision that did not bestow exclusive favoritism on the entity of man, but also covered the lamb that man so thoughtlessly subjected to the horror of fire, in a senseless ritual of sacrifice or in the beauty of a blade of grass that was trodden underfoot. In expounding these compassionate tenets, he made attempt to instill a realization that all things are the children of an expansive God; that the virtue of compassion alone could abolish man's inhumanity to man; his acts of brutality and only man himself, through a love of man, could establish a true state of salvation, as He gave up His mortal life, to imprint this truth on the mind of humanity forever.

"But we are afraid that as Christian doctrine, backed by the power of Rome, embarked on its composite of preceding cosmologies; His comprehension of understanding; the great depth of wisdom in His teachings were lost to the diffusion of selfishness as man, once again, sought to possess a private god for his own specific little sphere, with the sword or torture rack, to all non believers. Surely as foreign to Christ as He was to the bits of wood and stone that had been carved, in a version of God, before His coming.

"And now I have probably talked way past your supper time which will be corrected in that restaurant, just ahead."

We were seated in a cozy little booth with a lighted candle in the center of the table that had accumulated a tremendous build up of wax drippings and the soft glow of its flickering flame created an atmosphere of warmth and friendship that seemed so fitting as this wonderful day was drawing to its close. During supper Zret remarked, "I have taken several hours to answer just four or your questions and in a rather schematic pattern, at that, but it should give you a fair impression as to thoroughness in which I intend to teach and although you may not fully comprehend or remember all that I have said today; if you are still deeply interested in my promise of a complete knowledge, the future hours that we spend together I shall number among the more enjoyable of my life."

I do not believe I will ever feel closer to "my stranger" than at this moment and told him I doubted if I could forget even one word that he had spoken today for archeology and paleontology were fascinating subjects to me and I had studied many of Dad's architectural books, which carried one back to early Egypt, its Pyramids, temples and mummies; to classic Greece and Rome; was familiar with the philosophies of Plato and Aristotle; enjoyed reading Homer and in the past have spent many hours in the museums of Art and Natural History, in New York, for my quest of knowledge seems unquenchable and from our discussion today, I feel sure that you can fill in the missing links and gaps of our recorded history. It will be with the greatest eagerness that I look forward to seeing you again and hope that the intervals will not be too long.

"But before leaving me off at home tonight, there is one question that I wish you would answer. My brother is studying aviation and I have pumped him regarding various type airplanes and from his answers the only principle in existence that could lift a heavier than air vehicle, in take off, is an engine and propeller except, under certain conditions, the air currents that sustain a slow and unpredictable glider and it requires quite a wing span. Ever since you took off in that little round disc I have been trying to figure how it works and the only thing that comes to mind is a rifle, in principle.

"You can see the bullet when inserted into the magazine but once you pull the trigger, it disappears through a tremendous velocity in leaving the muzzle, just as you disappeared in a split second and I know that you did not evaporate for I watched your ship move very slowly across the river the night that you paused overhead. Another thing, how do you take up, I guess it would be called, the recoil?; for all guns kick and even a sudden start of an automobile presses one back against the seat or in a quick stop you may go through the windshield. To keep me from going nutty trying to fathom out these mysteries; what really makes your little ship fly? How do you anchor yourself inside? Will you ever take me for a ride?"

He studied me for at least a full minute and replied, "You know very well where your questions lead and even if there was time this evening to answer them, I am not at liberty to disclose the many mathematical details involved, in the operation of our ships but can ease your mind with a few examples of action and reaction resulting from natural force.

"The planet on which we are sitting, in its flight around the sun, travels more than a half billion miles at high velocity in one year, but does it have an engine and propeller?

"Let's see, how do I anchor myself in? This one has a bit of a quizzical twist but does show some deep thinking on your part and you probably also formed a mental picture of me being splattered all over the inside of my ship and rather than quote the slightly dull routine of figures, I will illustrate with an amusing but wholly understandable representation.

"Suppose that you took a juicy apple pie and without removing it from the cardboard plate, scaled it into the air; what would happen? Just as you visualized should happen to me, in motivation of your query: the plate would sail in one direction, the crust scatter about and the juicy apples inside splatter over everything because each component is traveling as a disconnected and separate entity, reacting in their own specific way to force and velocity. The same reactive principle that effects a person riding in an automobile, plane, etc.

"So, in another supposition, a similar fragile pie is frozen solid in its plate and scaled. It will glide a bit before hitting the ground, bounce or roll and come to rest intact, for each of its components has been moving, as a whole and although we are not frozen in our ships, this same state of synchronized unity is achieved through a method of fusing ship and crew as an integral mass, for if they traveled as separate entities, the extreme velocities that we may employ in take off or the slightest angle of deviation or complete turn from a straight line, in flight, would pulverize any human against his seat or on the walls of the ship.

"I realize this is not a very scientific explanation but the principles involved are, at least, contemporary and should keep you from going nutty. Under certain rulings imposed, in coming to your planet, we are not permitted to allow anyone, except of our race, to even enter the ships, for a negative condition could possibly arise, so a ride will have to await some future day if or when this ruling should ever be revised.

"And now young man it is after 9 o'clock and your mother, as my adopted one, are probably starting to worry about us, so finish your coffee for this delightful day must inevitably come to a close and that time has just about arrived."

Thus was my formal or shall I correctly state, very informal introduction to an inconceivable race of people and the wealth of knowledge endowed to me by this one of its members; the seemingly unbelievable facts that he has revealed, I cannot doubt, for so many of the topics in his teachings are now being confirmed by our own research. In all my lifetime I will never be as impressed with any invention, as my first glimpse of that little round disc standing on its three legs, in the clearing of a wilderness, forty-six years ago.

The impression in my mind is as vivid today, as the moment I stood in open mouthed wonder and watched it whisk away, to become enveloped in the blue of the sky.

CHAPTER 4
ZRET TALKS OF HIS ANCESTORS

About six weeks had passed since our trip to Lake Mahopac, when Zret called on the telephone to tell me that he had not forgotten next Friday was the anniversary of our meeting and this one special day of the year would become a must in our get-togethers. So, to meet him in the lobby of the McAlpine at 6:30, to initiate the first of these annual celebrations.

We had a most enjoyable dinner at the Brevoort and spent a good part of the evening swapping tales of camping and fishing experiences, for his love of the outdoors, of nature and the wilderness was as deep and compelling as my own. Some descriptions of the lakes and streams, in the heart of Canada, that he had been able to visit by using his little ship, stirred quite a yen inside of me, for in many he doubted that a white man had ever before cast a fly. In the course of the conversation he asked, 'no extended trip this year?' I said no, that I was taking an art course this summer, so would have to confine my trips to the weekends.

"Fine," he remarked, "for I had a thought in the back of my mind to suggest one for next weekend. Have you made any other plans?" Our meetings were so rare and far between that I would have cancelled a date, even with my best girl and arrangements were made to meet next Saturday at the Palisades Boat Club where I kept my canoe.

We paddled up the Hudson to one of my favorite camping sites just above Croton that had a good spring and on the other side of the river was some excellent hiking terrain and good fishing spots in the foothills of the Catskills. After setting up camp, we crossed the river to spend an exhilarating day of tramping and fishing and Zret's explanations of many plant specie origins and the benefits of insect kingdoms was an absorbing lesson in biology, to which we seldom give a passing thought. It was about 6:30 when we recrossed the river and our string of yellow perch tasted like a banquet, for I was as hungry as a bear.

After supper we stretched out in front of the campfire and Zret said, "Tonight I am going to take you on an imaginary journey in a Norca Ship that will carry us 20,000 years back in time and far into the great void of space, some seventy million, million miles from our solar system to a planet, once endearingly called 'Norca', that orbits the star you know as Tau Ceti and in a related story, from the archives of our history, we will relive an incredible saga of a very ancient and highly advanced race of beings, my ancestors, who dwelled on this planet.

"Before embarking on this visionary journey a few explanations would be in order to enable a clearer definition, a better understanding of conditions that existed in creating the whys and wherefores of their unfolding story, as our great ship would have approached their solar system, twenty thousand years ago. You recall our last discussion and my mention of the Universal Nucleus, its pulsation and effect on all solar systems in a general locale, on the spiral arms or perimeters of a galaxy, as they reach a direct line proximity of 'High Noon' on our mythical galactic clock, causing land and climate inversion, Major Glaciation periods, etc. To be more specific the Nucleus is a tremendous vehicle of motion, comprising pure energy and at absolute zero.

"A tremendous energy outpouring gives birth to the electron and proton at its face and as they are bent into the magnetic lines of force, surrounding the Nucleus, their mating creates the Hydrogen Atoms, foundation blocks of all matter for through a fusion by synthesis, the primal suns are formulated, then suns and planets in the eventual grouping of galaxies. In this action of synthesis and the suns of the galaxies they form, will be found the only 'Heat' in the Universe. The great ice ages occur in this closer proximity to the Nucleus, because a spiral arm is pulled out to its farthest extreme from the bulk of the galaxy and the average sun is not hot enough to completely offset this direct impact of its icy breath.

"During a good part of this era a majority of the snowfall and ice that builds up on a planet, in winter, does not thaw with the advent of summer and over thousands of years grow into the gigantic glaciers that cover its surface as they slowly creep toward the equator.

"But even an ice age does not persist in methodical order throughout its span and is an erratic in manner, as the countless other deviations that materialize in galactic rotation, under the unpredictable influence that the pulsations of the Nucleus exerts. This pulsation is not a rhythmic cycle, such as the tick of a clock or a heartbeat, but sporadic eruptions in a thousand or thousands of year spasms due to apparent colossal internal upheaval and the resulting extreme in its outpouring of energy, not only force an outward bending of the magnetic warps, in which a galaxy travels, but also the intensification in the clouds of hydrogen, when assimilated by a sun, will tend to raise its temperature, creating the oscillations or warming trends that occur during all of these glaciation eras.

"A simple illustration of this reaction may be induced by the glowing embers of our campfire; apply a bellows and it will flare up in rising temperature, warming up the spot where we are now sitting; stop the pumping and it will return to the original heat of its even burning. In a similar action of a stepped up sun's heat, the ice starts to melt in a recession of glacial movement that raises its own particular brand of havoc on a suffering planet, with floods of melt water and torrential rains, ripping and tearing up its land.

"But as these upheavals, within the nucleus subside, the magnetic warps conform to their typical paths, may even bend inward a bit which can bring on added woes, as the energy flux resumes its steadier flow, the suns cool to near normal temperatures and the ice on their planets again starts building in glacial advance, until the rotation of the galaxy carries their specific locale beyond this direct pull of the Nucleus.

"Then in a gradual contraction these solar systems move back, in closer affinity to the galaxies bulk, enabling the normal heat of their suns to control the formation of ice, as the glaciers slowly recede toward the poles of a planet.

"These major glaciation periods occur on all water bearing planets that are close enough to the heat of their suns, to at least maintain a partial liquid state in the water content of their lakes, rivers and seas under temperate conditions and brings into stark reality just one of the adversities that establishes a limbo of extinction to many plant and animal orders.

"As I mentioned previously, they appear in approximate two hundred twenty-three million year spans, regulated by one revolution of the galaxy and their duration also fluctuates, from just over a million years of the latest one, that we have so recently survived, to over six million years in some past incidences. The mathematics of these unstable timetables I will explain as your studies advance, but it will give you a fair idea of reasons that contribute to the demise of a planet's life complexes and as I recount the subsequent course of action taken by my ancestors, during our mental flight back into history, you will be fully aware of the fearful odds that the human brain can overcome when science is applied to the benefit of preservation of life.

"Does this orient your mind as to how the planets would have appeared? Earth, with its mantle of ice, as it glides around the Sun and Norca in an icy sheath circling Tau Ceti, just as innumerable others were doing in this immediate vicinity, when our story opens?"

I said, "Yes, I think that it can picture winters thousands of years long, with icebergs stretching out all over the place, for I saw one from the boat, when we were coming back home from England, just before the war started in 1914 and I know the destruction that a spring thaw can cause just from one winter, but does the ice ever reach the equator?"

"Only on far our planets that have sufficient water to build that much ice or those in the eternity of chemical ice," he replied, "and it does not happen to planets with deep oceans that are as close to their suns as Earth, for the warmth of these waters helps to retard a complete cover and also the warming trends intervene.

"However there is one exception when a former equatorial region may become part of an ice field, in the not too frequent inversion that causes the poles of a planet to shift position, thereby creating a new equator and it has happened more than once in Earth's long history.

"Now, as we have a cup of coffee and add a couple of

logs to our campfire, I will proceed to turn back time and if you were amazed at my little ship, standing in the wilderness, I cannot conceive what your emotions would have been as you gazed at a veritable circular mountain of gleaming metal, thirty-two thousand feet in diameter with its central dome as tall as the Woolworth Building, for this was a Norca ship of advanced design and none being anywhere near Earth at that period, we will skip across the void of time and distance, to join its crew in their control complex, as they are heading home from an experimental flight that will terminate in about a year and a half.

"I have chosen this ship and its particular position, in becoming imaginary members of her compliment, so that you may gain a broader comprehension of the vast stretches of emptiness surrounding even a single sun and give added credence to a statement that I have previously made, regarding all the matter in the Universe representing less than one percent of its whole, as, in traveling to this solar system I will portray in words, the impression of observation, through which you will also see some of the creative wonders, born of the human brain and the phenomena in nature.

"We now find ourselves seated in the nerve center of this great ship and before strolling about to peer over the shoulders of the various engineers, in their routine check of its operational functions, I will explain a few of the panels, screens, meters and dials that comprise a major part of this control area. The large panel directly ahead, with the streaks of light and zig zagging lines crossing its surface, is the receiving core for all information gathered by the impulse grids and scanners, whose electronic fingers constantly probe the reaches of a cosmos and this data is transposed and evaluated by the internal mechanism of this panel, feeding to the appropriate instruments of reception.

"Through the series of fifty panels on the left, that appear to have a pale milky glass in their frames, various electron intensities materialize in visual pattern and the forty frames on the right, with slightly smoky looking faces, relay light rays in color and conformity of their original emission, just as though you were watching a motion picture in the true hues of nature. The banks of dials, meters, etc., that stretch along the lower part of the wall, number fifteen hundred in all and record in electronic blocks or units calculated from the vibrational frequency of a specific atom and those that we examine, I will translate into the standard tables of time, velocity and round figures, used by your particular country on earth.

"With this general acclimation we will join the engineers to determine our exact location and distance from Tau Ceti. The speed of our ship, expected time of arrival at this destination and how these factors are established. If you will look at the left second panel from the bottom, you will see on its milky face, a large prominent black dot and obliquely encircling it, in odd spacing, seven lesser dots. That panel is one of the visual indicator screens of the ship's synchronized guidance system and the dots are electromagnetic impressions of Tau Ceti and its seven planets.

"The dial that we are now approaching calculates the energy formulating the dots on the screen at this moment, was emitted by the sun, Tau Ceti, four months ago and the meter above it registers the energy's velocity at one hundred eighty-six thousand miles a second, confirming our present location as two million, million miles from its source. As you glance to the right, this dial records the decreasing time that it takes the energy leaving Tau Ceti to create the dots on the screen and in the ten seconds that we have been watching, its meter recording this span has decreased by three hundred eighty thousand miles, establishing the speed of our ship at thirty-eight thousand miles per second or just a fraction over one-fifth the velocity of light.

"The meter below shows that at this constant velocity, our objective will be reached in the approximate round figures of nineteen months and three weeks. If our ship were headed toward Earth, traveling at this tremendous speed, it would take about sixty years to make the trip. I believe in this time-velocity ratio you will recognize the incredible distances that separate the suns, and these two are relatively close in galactic dimension.

"And now we will move over to view the screens on the right, that are receiving light rays and more understandable than the electronic impressions of this group for you will be able to see the suns, gas clouds, constellations, etc., on which their scanners are focused. The first one I will point out is the frame on the upper right tier, that resembles the picture of a piece of black velvet with some of its pile rubbed the wrong way. The blackness that appears as velvet is a minute part of the void of space within our own galaxy and it would take the ship ten thousand years to reach the vicinity of the faintly luminous streaks of bluish haze; that is actually a gigantic cloud of ionized gas and cosmic dust stretching for millions of miles in formative stage, that will eventually compress and generate sufficient heat energy to evolve into a new sun.

"On the screen at the end of the middle row you will observe a circular tilted disc that has the aspects of a pinwheel rolling along on edge, just about ready to fall over. This is another spiral galaxy, closest to our own system in distance and of the same approximate size and constitution. If it were in the realm of possibility, a trip to its fringes would take us almost seven million years and the space in between is empty, except for the primal energy of electrons and protons.

"In analyzing its structure you will note its brilliant center or core, slightly resembling the yolk of a fried egg, sunny side up, comprising billions of its very hot primal suns, and the dark streaks and holes in this area are caused by sun explosion and gas venting that occur at intervals throughout its lifetime. The millions of bright globules that fan out concentrically are suns and planets that form its massive curving arms and only on some planets of the suns that comprise these arms will you find life materialization compatible to our own.

"As we study these spiral arms, the suns in the arm curling around the lower edge of the galaxy are more compact, closer to its bulk, for they are shielded from the direct influence of the Nucleus, while the arm curving around its upper edge, extends outward considerably and a number of its suns pulled so far away, that they do not even appear to be part of the arm and some never do return.

"This is a reaction to the Nucleus which I have explained and reason that the crust of certain planets crinkles into mountain ranges and major glaciation periods emerge, for this top edge is facing the Nucleus and in identical position to the arm of our galaxy, in which the sun of Earth and Tau Ceti are located. Although the astronomical distance of over a million light years separates these two galaxies, many of the planets of these suns are experiencing the same throes of icing that is effecting us.

"In looking at the lower arm we may recapture a picture of how the location of our present suns and planets appeared over a half galactic revolution ago and this shielded era varies from ninety to one hundred ten million years, as to the entrance and departure of a specific sun and its planets. The initial phase of this close swing in may institute a very minor icing period that extends just below a planet's polar caps, but as this long era progresses, the ice gradually disappears, sporadic torrential rains create enormous lake chains and endless swamps, the water levels of its seas will rise and as a planet adjusts to this changing pattern, its mountains erode into low rolling hills and the mild climate, without appreciable temperature variation between winter and summer, becomes an ideal environment for all the plant life and established creatures of a habitable planet.

"This condition was the stimulus to the long reign of Earth's cold blooded Dinosaurs and the budding of newer forms, that eventually led to the mammal, as the adversity of later epochs advanced this warm blooded specie to its branchings of higher animal orders. If you will look closely at this arm, whose major structure is tucked so snugly around the galaxies lower edge, you will notice a gap or loosening at its base that is emerging from behind the galaxy's bulk and as its rotation continues, the arm will swing further out under influence of the Nucleus and when our specific planet approaches this point, which in an earlier description I implied as Dawn, its temperature will differentiate sharply, into the distinction of Winter and Summer.

"As the swing out becomes more pronounced, mountains will again build up and a minor glaciation period ensues, with its ice robbing a considerable amount of water from the lakes and seas, just another incidence in the many that spells finis to older plant and animal orders. For instance, the dinosaur and its contemporary, much of the swamp and marine life, entire groupings of fern life, various aggregations of conifers, etc.

"These group extinctions, or in your thinking, the entrance to the state of death do not necessarily mean the end of matter, reverting to its gases of origin, but over hundreds of millions of years these upheavals, faults opening that swallow entire water bodies, enfolding earth and rock, covering land, swamp and sea bottom, buries portions of these populations and through tremendous weight pressure and chemical decomposition, will directly convert these former living organisms into other type of matter. Still later upheaval exposes or brings them closer to the surface, in new garb and some of these forms, a very useful utility to modern man, as he mines or otherwise reclaims them from the limbo of their past.

"The tiny protozoan that swarms in the seas and silt of their bottoms, reappear as marble, chalks, limestone, etc., that are used to form the columns and walls of a temple, cut into the erection blocks of building or ground into the adhesive of constructions cement.

The color and beauty of the ferns, the plant and trees that once so gracefully raised their slender branches into the atmosphere, toward the energy of a sun, now compressed to the black carbon mineral solid of extensive coal beds. Marine life that cavorted in the waters, the land and swamp creatures that played, loved or fought in these compatible environs, repose as deep pockets of crude oil, with which the ingenuity of a human brain, warms his home, turns the wheels of industry, powers a ship, automobile or airplane, through an exothermic action of their energy's release.

"Even though they again seem to vanish, during these processes, as the coal bin soon empties and must be refilled, just as happens to the gasoline tank of your automobile, but the expelling of these energies through a combining with oxygen, creates diversifying forms of matter represented in the exhaust gas of carbon monoxide, carbon dioxide, sulphur dioxide, etc., which will blend in structural harmony with other materialization. So you see there is really no permanence of design in either applied term of life or death, but only stages that depict the evolution of energy in its restless flight of unceasing motion.

"The last screen we will examine tonight is the third frame to the right in this same row that shows a fiery spheroid on a jet black background, and the rays formulating this true life photograph were emitted by this radiant ball seven thousand million light years in the past. In other words, it has taken this almost unbelievable time, distance span for these impressions to travel through the void of the universe and what is now appearing on this screen is its form and character, as in those countless eons ago that may overawe the ability of the brain to interpret, in an absolute sense.

"What you are watching is an unborn galaxy in a late stage of its evolution comprising the energy and gases of billions of primal suns. It is rolling free and in spurts, will sometimes attain close to the velocity of light, may cross lines of magnetic force and if it does not catch up to or sideswipe another established galaxy of a specific warp, the tremendous internal pressure will eventually expand with explosive force to scatter huge globules of super heated gas and energy in every direction from its perimeter and in this phase will then stabilize in this reactive warp of convenience, to take its place in the universe as a new galaxy with its sun structures, planets and perhaps evolve life in our familiar patterns should it mature as a spiral.

"The viewing of this one entity has a little story attached to it, for a scanner on all of their ships and several in home based observatories had maintained a constant fix on its impression over several thousands of years as each generation hoped that they would be the honored ones to witness and record this birth of a galaxy.

"This closing description will also close your lessons, for it is time to turn in, but have you been able to visualize this ship and its control room, the pictures that I have painted with an oral brush?

(I was so engrossed that I seemed to actually sit in front of those screens, watch as each dial and meter was scrutinized by the engineers and my one wish in the composing of this book, is to be as fluid, as vivid in portrayal, in my conveyance of the images he has imprinted on my memory.)

I could only reply that I had lived each moment with a definite pattern of the universe starting to formulate in my mind and regretted that time flies so swiftly, for I was really not tired, but he reminded me that tomorrow is another day and as we sleep, our great ship will continue her journey, just as she will eternally fly, in thought and the annals of racial history, the forerunner of a fleet that would someday blaze a path across the void, as they sought a new home, new hope in the unknown surroundings of a strange solar system and through the unfathomable mechanics of destiny, was to be the only ship to survive this fateful flight.

"So under the blankets for us and in the morning, as we fish the river in a drifting canoe, will rejoin her for a tour of inspection, just before conclusion of this experimental flight and to later witness an inexorable trend of nature, reclaim her essentials to the gift of life. In a picturization of this factual reclamation you will fully realize that in all the cosmos only the inventive genius of a human brain may temporarily parry or ultimately devise a means of salvation, through escape, as the veil of oblivion descends to enshroud a former joyful, living world forever.

STARFALL · I SAVED THE LIFE OF A SPACE ALIEN

Panels of a Space Ship Control Center

In the early 1920's, when these panels were originally described to me, it was a bit beyond my complete understanding. At that time our science was in a very primal stage of radio development. Radar, television, radio telescopes, light splitting devices, computers and many of the electronic marvels that today are taken for granted; not even a remote thought in the mind of the layman. Over years of Zret's teaching and our arrival to some of the principles embodied in this control center, it became very clear that the great central panel was a highly specialized computer to automatically control every action of the ship, its force fields, gravitational and electromagnetic fields. The "scanners," not only the eyes of a guidance system; but also put the Universe at the finger tips of its operators. Truly an amazing feat of electronic wizardry.

CHAPTER 5
TAU CETI AND NORCA

The sun had not yet peeped over the low lying hills to the east, when breakfast was sizzling in the pan and coffee brewing, for the early morning hours are a fisherman's paradise and were not to be wasted in sleep. With the inner being satisfied, we soon pushed off, to paddle a few miles up river and from there to drift and cast in our enjoyable pastime.

I could not actually determine whether the pleasure of fishing or desire to continue our discussion of last evening, predominated my thinking, but the combination of both surely promised a perfect day. The methodical dip, gurgle, dip, as our paddles bit into the water's surface, seemed to render a tonal zest of excitement to this dual anticipation of adventure on the rivers bosom and continuance of a visionary flight through the void of space.

"You are almost thinking out loud." Zret's voice cut into my thoughts, "As I too, have been lost in the enchantment of the river, with the dawning of a new day and cannot but wonder, how long, this heritage of beauty that nature so lavishly entrusted to the custody of Earthman, will endure. I have watched the green mantles of her hills and forests converted into the green of dollar bills, her sparkling waters thoughtlessly desecrated by pollution of population and industry, because it is a convenient and 'economical' means of disposal, the birds and magnificence of her wildlife on land and in the sea, decimated, for profit or sport.

"There is a salient fact that comes to the fore, as we contemplate these actions and perhaps nature, in bringing forth man, may have created one of the greater potentials of destructive force in the universe, if sadistic motivation is coupled to mental genius. Should this profusion be smothered, allowed to dwindle away to this god of profit, without even a guide line of wisdom, where then will he turn? The planets of this solar system will remain fruitful for many millions of years, but the brain of man could change it in a day and as we go back in time, you will fully realize the utter desolation of a treeless landscape, without bird, animal, insect, when an aging sun and its planets naturally lose their ability to sustain this bounty of life. It is a sorrowful sight, even under the inevitability of age, but how much more tragic, when engineered by the full and vigorous breath of life itself, in the guise of man?

"In rejoining our ship, for the promised tour of inspection, you will enter a strange, but fascinating miniature world of a simulated planet and although, not in exact image, the brain of man has created all but one cardinal requisite that maintains the flow of life in a customary environment of its origin. His genius has improved on nature in breaking the natural planetary restrictions of dependency on a sun, in fixed orbit, as we now cruise far beyond its influence and through navigational instrumentation, may return at will.

"But nature, in turn, has placed a restriction on man in a limitation of the distance that he may travel and still survive, for throughout his scientific research and invention, he has not devised a means to artificially produce, in any great quantity, the vital ingredient of existence, water. He has, however, extended the duration of survival in this type ship with a full compliment to several decades through reconstituting method of gases, chemical and water, but ultimately must depend on a water bearing planet, for replenishment of supply.

"This manifestation is peculiar only to certain planets, in compatible placement to a sun, with its appearance and continuance dependent on mass, thermal mechanics, gravitational forces and energy synchronization between planet and sun, in any given solar system. An excellent example of these trends may be gained, in an analysis of Mars and Earth, two of the three water bearing planets of this system. The location, bulk and dynamics of Earth are ideal in producing and retention of abundant water in its atmosphere and seas for an extended period of time, still a depreciation is evident in our thirteen thousand years of record.

"Mars, on the other hand, although farther out and smaller than Earth, does come within this required standard of mass, etc., to originally bring forth a quite plentiful accumulation but its lesser bulk and in ratio, dynamics, were unable to prevent the escape of a major portion of this moisture, from its atmosphere and surface. Smaller natural planets, even in favorable placement to a specific sun, do not have the ability to even build up or hold the chemical vapor that could establish an atmosphere or condense on their crusts, as water.

"In momentarily side tracking our tour, I believe that you will have a clearer understanding of the tremendous forces involved and why this huge ship must carry its own water supply, but we do hope that the everlasting probe of man's mind will someday surmount this problem and the research of science, solve the riddle of lesser dynamics, in creation of this precious fluid. In a realm of possibility it could also open the way to penetrate the fringes of infinity.

"So we will again delve into these infinite reaches of the mind as memory in bridging the mists of time return us to the familiar control room and by walking through the opening opposite the panels wall emerge in the corridor of a circular complex four hundred and eighty feet in diameter, the exact center and magnetic pole area of the ship. Forty feet from the metallic wall through which we have just entered is a transparent partition four hundred feet in diameter housing its heart of energy cells which generate all electronic impulse, electromagnetic fields, gravitational fields, stabilization, velocity potential, etc. If you will look through this enclosure... ."

At this point I interjected a question, "Is this partition made of glass?"

"No," he replied, "its structure is composed of several super heated gases and combining under compression in these intense thermal energies, this solidified product has the clarity of glass, but its durability and strength is a thousand times that of steel.

"And now, in looking through, you can imagine a massive, highly polished needle, fifty feet in diameter and its length exactly seven times this thickness, that is set in a semi gyroscopic mounting, but unlike a gyroscope's free running pivotal axis, its frame is centrally fixed in conjunction with a track that encircles the enclosure.

"This needle is spinning in synchronization with the ship's revolving perimeter edge, creating various magnetic fields and major forces of its operational performance. For instance, the rate of spin in its present vertical position governs the ship's velocity, and the slight wobble that may be noticed occasionally, is due to its stabilizing influence. If the needle was positioned on a transverse plane, an inversion of polarity will hold the ship motionless and an induction or regulated displacement of electrons, while in this plane, would enable the ship to vertically rise or descend, the velocity in either direction again controlled by the needle's rate of spin.

"I know this must sound like Greek to you now, but as we study the higher mathematics of the universe, understanding will clarify its entire motivation by electronic energy, formation of electromagnetic fields of like and opposing polarities and, through a compression of these magnetic fields, an energy conversion of tremendous proportion takes place. In applying this principle of energy conversion to many of his everyday needs man also advances his lot in life. If, in the future, you may have the opportunity to observe one of our ships coming in for a landing, or taking off, you will notice a conspicuous little flutter characteristic in all, whether large or small, for our present ships are still patterned in the same principle as a Norca Ship.

"Regardless of angle we may approach a landing site, a momentary pause is required to touch down vertically and of course the initial phase of ascent, a vertical lift. The positional shift of the needle, that I have described, from vertical to a horizontal plane or visa versa, causes this characteristic little flutter motion of a ship during this operation and I believe this explanation will clear away a bit of your mystery of how my little ship flies.

I remembered the flutter, as his ship momentarily paused and the legs folded into the recesses of its bottom, after rising about thirty feet above ground, on the first morning of our meeting. A strike interrupted the discourse and I watched him deftly manipulate his rod, in slow easy motion maneuvering the fish to the canoe's side, then reach into the water and release it with a few words of advice, "Maybe this will instill a little caution, for next time you may not be as lucky."

Somehow these incidents still seemed to touch on the unreal, an ageless man, with the universe at his finger tips, deriving so much pleasure in the simplicity of playing a fish on the end of a line, yet, just as happy watching it dart away, free again and alive.

The sequence of fact and flowing word blending into dreamlike structure; I can still see myself, one short year ago, picking a way over log and rock, the muffled cry in the wilderness, a little deed of compassion, a pledge and, like Aladdin rubbing his lamp, a new world opens. An unknown race of people, apparently on some secret mission that comes under the heading of mercy, without thought of glory or compensation, only because their philosophy teaches an encompassing love, not solely to the being of man but for the blade of grass, an insect, the water and trees.

The very limited acquaintance—only four meetings—but doubt cannot take root in my mind for the fantastic picturizations anchor on fact. A flying suit and its panel explain a dying man's initial adamant refusal of aid. The fluttering and disappearance of an unearthly little ship that I had touched, watched, described by its mechanism the sun, stars and planets are real. Perhaps the boundless wonders that are starting to unfold as true comprehension widens may even define the question he never actually answered and the elusive "Heaven" that man eternally seeks, to be revealed in the wisdom of knowledge.

Musing again, Zret said, "For I can hear the wheels turning in your head. What are you really thinking?"

"Oh! Just sort of reviewing the past year and still cannot come to the full realization, whether it is a dream and maybe a little bit afraid that I may awaken before it ends, for many things are so utterly strange. Things that cannot be connected with anything that I have ever studied or even read about and fixed impressions are hard to displace while others have always been confusing.

"Your age for instance. I have studied paintings by Michelangelo, those of others portraying Biblical Prophets and even as in the myth of Rip Van Winkle great age, in my mind, has always been associated with snowy hair and long white beards, yet you, perhaps several times their age, appear as a boy. Bible history set creation of the universe at less than six thousand years ago, with man coming forth as a completed entity and woman made from his rib. But according to your galactic clock, elemental man evolved from a lower animal order more than sixteen million years ago.

"I have also read of heaven and in confliction the Tower of Babel being struck down because of man's presumption to reach it, giving support to a theory that it is some where just above the clouds. Then again Greek legend tells of Icarus, in escaping from Crete on wings made by his father of feathers and wax, foolhardily flying so close to the sun that the wax melted and he fell to his death in the sea. I know that the sun is millions of miles away but although there is much confusion in our history, these things do stick in the mind.

"Now I learn from you of great ships, like flying cities, for I have figured six miles across times pi is almost nineteen miles around their edges and travelling at the incredible speed of thirty-eight thousand miles per second, to the remote reaches of another sun, long before the world was supposed to have been created. But these things that you have taught me to see—formation of suns, other galaxies, their reaction to the Nucleus of the Universe, cause and effect on life and why it vanishes, time spans—that you do not relate from a misty background of legend or the supposition of maybe and perhaps, but in an apparent actuality of their proven existence and as I cannot find any reason why you should fool me, disbelief will not cloud my mind, only the thought that it could be just a dream."

"No," said Zret, "it is not a dream in the sense of unreality, and many times since our meeting, I have also wondered, is it a lingering thread from out of the past, as I teach an earthling? Your extreme youth, have I been wise? Did sentiment run away with caution? But the characteristic, your trends of thought, are so very much like my own and the readiness that you grasp and accept description, just as though refreshing a memory stir a baffling intangible within me that leaves the feeling of something far deeper between us than a new found bound of friendship or the sentiment of gratitude. I know 1 will never regret my decision of teaching and am sure you will eventually accept these lessons in the truth that they represent. We both have had ample time to appraise and I cannot find skepticism in your reaction but only a very understandable dilemma in the confliction of analogy.

"Time will be the ultimate adjuster, so we will leave these little problems behind and continue our tour of the ship. As you have calculated, the outer edge is just over nineteen miles around with the inner circumference two miles shorter, the intervening mechanism and its revolving perimeter. It would be quite a hike to even cover the twenty-four square miles of its lower level where a variety of the more interesting experiments are being conducted, so we will utilize a transportation vehicle and in leaving the central circular corridor a descending ramp curves right to enter a twenty-one hundred acre tract of scientifically designed farm and pasture land. Many tests are in progressive stages of control, the soil is complete with bacteria, animalcules and surface insects, both friend and foe to plant life with the only difference that if natural balance becomes offset by a predominant specie, its proliferation is curtailed by electronic or chemical check on its ability to reproduce.

"To the left are fields of wheat, barley and corn, rows of squash, legumes, including types of soy bean, potatoes and beet root. To the right, pasture land and the golden brown cows grazing there are bred solely for milk production and somewhat smaller in stature than your dairy cows. The small animals grazing with them are antelope. The sheep in the next field are raised for their wool only and the horse corral is beyond. These magnificent animals are the pride of the various branches of science and the keenness of competition is intense as they vie for the honors of showmanship and in racing.

"As you glance around you will notice honey bees buzzing among the clover blossoms and in the flowers bordering the two small streams that cut through the pasture. Along the ship's walls, in this area, are milking stations, research compounds, laboratories and equipment manufacturing facilities.

"Adjacent to the farm lands are nine hundred acres planted with berry bushes and orchards of apple and plum, some in flower, others bearing fruit. The two streams continue through the orchard, there is an occasional growth of water cress and a trout like fish may jump for a fly. The bright bits of plumage that dart about the landscape represent, in major part, the basic seed eating finches and the insect and worm eating thrush families of the bird world. The artifical lighting effect produces identical benefit of light, heat and energy, as emitted by a native sun to give a feeling of the true outdoors and it is difficult to realize that you are travelling through space at the incredible velocity of thirty-eight thousand miles a second.

"Beyond the orchard we will enter a two thousand acre plant life processes of photosynthesis absorbing carbon dioxide and expelling oxygen. All these trees are of the genus coniferae, a gymnospermae group, whose exposed seeds mass together in various configurations of a cone and very similar to the pines, cedars and yews of earth. One stream terminates here in quite a large pond, teeming with research specimens of aquatic life and is surrounded with ferns and rushes.

"An adjoining pool is an algae development conservation. Bridal paths wind through the trees; you may glimpse an antelope and tree climbing birds of the woodpecker family along with the finches and thrush as we travel through this idyllic setting to emerge in what I will infer as the city area of the ship.

"We first see a magnificent arena race track fashioned in a breath taking splendor of architectural excellence, with the remaining stream tracing patterns through the exotic floral design of the infield, to terminate in a small lake beyond its confines. Located here are housing facilities for twenty-two hundred families, theaters, athletic fields and archery ranges, all conforming in a motif of beauty that so symbolizes this race of mine.

"Underneath the ground or floor of this entire sixteen thousand acre lower level is a water reservoir and another in the topmost level of the ship. The intermediate levels house much of its mechanisms, manufacturing potentials, electronic doctoring center for physical malfunction, food and clothing distributing shops, etc.

"I have tried to convey a verbal visualization of the animals, the trees, water and buildings of our miniature worlds and in recalling my example of the two apple pies, you may well imagine what would happen, through deviation of course, a sudden dip, rise or stop if these vehicles were designed in the principle of carriers, such as the automobile, airplanes or ships that ply the waters of your seas.

"My ancient ancestors were wizards in electronic genius and they worked out magnetic gravitational fields that flow in one line of motion in relation to the ship's direction and all entities synchronized or fixed in this stabilized field of equalizing pressure. Although it does not restrict a freedom of action, movement of any kind can only be achieved through moto-impulse of the entity itself.

"This is a more technical interpretation of the frozen pie. To expand in comprehension of comparison we will analyze the effects on all objects of a natural planet as they are synchronized in a gravitational field of rhythmic motion, with the major force exerted on an entity pulling downward or toward center of the planet. In a hypothetical illustration we will assume that it is high noon and you are standing in vertical posture, head up and feet down, relative to your specific spot on the plane of planet Earth.

"Because it is round and turning, your inclination of angle is constantly changing and in six hours or roughly six thousand two hundred and fifty miles later, you will be in a horizontal position, with head sticking straight out sideways. Another six hours or at midnight you will be in reversed vertical posture, feet up and head hanging straight down in space, add six more hours, to reach assumed dawn and you again attain a horizontal position and in return to the starting point of high noon, you are standing upright. In this twenty- four hour period you have travelled twenty-five thousand miles on the crust of a spinning planet, with its orbital velocity around the sun, at some sixty-six thousand, six hundred and sixteen miles an hour.

"Yet there is no sensation of motion or the constant

variation of attitude because you are an integral part of its whole, synchronized in its rhythmic motion and gravitational field. Although the feet are literally glued to the surface, after you learn to walk, there is little restriction to muscular power initiating voluntary movement, unless in the act of climbing a hill which requires added energy to compensate for the lift of your weight against its pull.

"But in a conjecture of possibility, should the planet suddenly change course or deviate in velocity, you would immediately become conscious of this alien force and even a momentary overpowering by this pressure would disorganize the stabilizing influence of a rhythmic field, as all things lose equilibrium to tumble helter skelter about.

"Our fields move as an integral segment of the navigational complex of the ship and superimposed on the unidirectional pull of a gravitational field, is a circling electromagnetic field and through unity of these two fields an evenly distributed pressure is exerted on all parts of every entity, animate or inanimate, under its influence. In essence, it reacts to identical practice as the adhesion of a solidified mass, but unlike the inflexibility of rigid structure, permits complete maneuverability about, as part and within an equalizing field of force, that prohibits the potential of counteracted balance by alien pressure regardless of directional or velocity changes of the ship, as you also normally walk on the surface of Earth part of its field of unidirectional force unaware of its rhythmic spinning in unison to methodical flight around the sun.

"Research, by the Human Brain, that led to the conception and creation of artificial planets, in violation to a natural tradition of planetary control by its sun, also revealed the necessity of devising method to equalize opposing force that builds up through the unrhythmic and alternate motion at high velocity. A requirement that is not essential to anchor static life and objects to the crust or integral mass of a natural planet that evolved in the unilateral flow of uninterrupted motion.

"This research also brought to light the startling fact that voluntary movement or moto impulse, of entities, is not a natural reaction to planetary physics but was invented by evolving animate form through unrelenting compulsion to the procurment of food. Most insects and animals have not even learned the knack of balance to stand upright and move without falling toward this gripping one way force. The probe of science cannot find one provision in planetary law to protect or stabilize the field of a moving object on its surface, for this very act of disconnected dynamics violates the fundamental characteristic of rhythmic motion. This is the reason that a turn made too fast will upset an automobile, or a sudden stop may find you heading through the windshield. Animate movement is the odd ball of planetary scheme, but the basic that gave impetus to development of the brain.

"Although rather schematic, I believe this descriptive tour will give you a workable knowledge of this ship of destiny and a more rounded understanding of the part that she and her later sister ships were to play in the salvation of a race. We should soon be nearing the end of her maiden voyage, so will return to the control room and watch the approach to Tau Ceti and landing on Norca, just ten years after take off on this experimental flight.

"In reentering the control room we will first check the meters that record our distance from Tau Ceti and find that they show it is six hundred and fifty million miles away, but that the ship is well within the influence of the solar system. Our present velocity can only be maintained for the next two hours, which will place us some three hundred and seventy-five million miles from Norca and from that point in momentum will gradually decrease until about fifty thousand miles from where our course will intersect the orbit of Norca we will be travelling at a speed of one hundred thousand miles an hour. This entire distance, which would normally take less than five hours to traverse in the void of the galaxy will stretch out to seventeen hours before landing time at our destination.

"Meanwhile we will sit and relax in front of the screens at the right which, as you remember, transmit their pictures through photons or light rays and on the three frames at the end of the bottom tier you may observe the pattern of this solar system and in the approach to our goal the materialization of planetary detail. In looking at the last frame you see this general view and will notice that we are coming in from a slight angle above Tau Ceti, that in this picture appears as a glowing ember with rosy tongues of flame curling around its profile and situated just below the center of this screen. The disc straight ahead, near the top of the frame, that looks in size like a shiny half dollar, is the seventh or outer planet Ahereeca whose orbital aphelion is eight hundred twenty-nine million miles and the mean distance of the other six planets graduating down to thirty-seven million miles for Ne-Neeca, the smaller and closest planet to the sun. As you glance around this concentric group, these planets have the appearance of seven small moons, shining in their darkened background.

"Ahereeca, directly behind but above the sun, is reflecting its light from her full face and the others in various phases from three quarter full, to half moon and crescents. These differing configruations of each planet are caused by our angle of approach as the screens are depicting reflected light. The four behind and to the sides of the sun have more of their surfaces exposed to its light, whereas the three on this side have a major part of their bulk between it and our position, so that we only pick up the light reflecting from parts of their rounded edges, thus transmitting this crescent like effect. The brilliant yellowish tinted crescent toward the lower left corner of the screen is Norca.

"The scanner of the next screen is focused on Norca and the little fingers of flame that appear in the upper right hand corner of the frame are from the arc of a tiny segment of Tau Ceti's photosphere that the wide angle of the scanners focal beam has picked up. Norca's mean orbit is eighty-five million miles from the sun and is about seven-eights the size of Earth or seven thousand miles in diameter.

"We are still too far distant to reveal any surface detail, but the dazzling crescent with its longer point curving around her top edge is an awe inspiring sight and the very faint luminescence or aura that continues from the tip of this long point around three quarters of her circumference does outline a sphere; this resulting from the diffused glow of its ice fields. If you watch very closely you will occasionally see four flickers of light beyond but following its curvature.

"These are the four moons of Norca, the larger and outer one, a natural moon, similar to your moon and the other three are mechanical bodies, products of man's brain, that were designed to curtail evaporation by retarding the fast moving molecules that steal away as atmospheric gas; to stimulate moisture and temper the sharp differential of night time cold and heat of the day that become part of a dying planet's physics, under duress of thinning atmosphere and escape of infra red light.

"It would be several hours before the ship veers down to the daylight side of Norca, her guidance system fixed on the beam of the landing fields beacons, so our visionary flight will speed through those intervening hours and as we view the next screen, she will be gliding over top of the North Pole of the planet sixty miles above its surface.

"The glare of the ice is quite intense but the horizontal curvature is very distinct and in proceeding southward our altitude and speed will gradually decrease as objects start to take form. The dark mounds and spears are mountains jutting through glacial fields, the yellowish tinge is mist rising from melting ice sheets, for the planet is still basking under the influence of a warming trend in this glaciation era. Directly below us now are edges of a receding frozen world and you can see great cascades of pale greenish yellow water tumbling down its sides and gushing from beneath ice field and glacier. The interspersed black rolling waves are storm clouds, pouring out their contingent, in torrential rain squalls; streams, lakes and shallow inland seas are the main pattern of the landscape, but the green of vegetation is becoming evident and then blends into the darker green of the forests.

"This belt is not too extensive and within four hundred miles we will pass over its ragged border line that appears as short fingers and peninsulars of fertile soil with its plant life protruding into the yellow brown dust, sand and rock of a desolate area that covers the entire equatorial zone, for it has long ago dehydrated. As we fly over this barren expanse there is not a blade of grass, a tree or an animal and the only movement to be detected, the spasmodic swirl of dust clouds in this arid, lifeless desert. But look, our scanner is picking up hundreds of smaller craft darting all around us, the first of a welcoming committee to honor this spectacular achievement.

"Our bearing is still due south and above the shimmering heat waves and haze of dust particles the low contours of a mountain range will take shape, the northern most extreme of Norca's southern hemisphere and the ship is almost home. Wooded rolling hills stretch beneath us, but this band is also narrow for the ice fields are not far beyond as they mass to southward, but adversity is not apparent here in this summertime period of glacial epoch.

"Our ship angles sharply down and a large lake comes into view, fed by a river that winds through the floor of its picturesque valley, the face of a great white cliff looms ahead and the valley opens to a sparkling jewel in an emerald setting; the City of Norma, larger of the three remaining towns of my ancient race and research center that created their symbol of hope in guise of this wonderful craft.

"The ribbon-like lines that interlace the countryside are, in simple terminology, highways over which glide their wheelless vehicles, cushioned on a magnetic field and similar to the one that we used on our tour. Journey's end is minutes away as we hover motionless seven hundred feet above the surface of her enormous landing field and you can see the buildings of the city terracing down the hillsides.

"Architecturally their design is circular, with tinted domed roofs and walls of pinkish white stone peculiar to this valley, their beauty enhanced with graceful curving arches and splashing fountains amid a profusion of flowers, each one decorated with banners and colored streamers in honor of this gala event.

"The ship slowly descends and just before touching down, a massive grid of electrodes that honeycomb the landing field's base will discharge her build up of static electricity and radiation; flashing blue and incandescent white flames race over her structure to arc on the electrodes below, a necessary action to eliminate all potential of harmful effect. Only then will Norca's meager population of seven hundred twenty-five thousand men, women, and children rush out from compounds of the field's vast perimeter to welcome and pay homage to a ship, the branches of science and scientists who resolved a dream of theory and diligence of research, into reality of successful test flight.

"In this detailed description you are probably aware of an oddity in extremes that couples the technology of a very highly advanced science and mastery of electronics that created these flying miniature worlds, with intimately planned phases of pastoral simplicity, reverting to primal impetus that grouped primitive man into communities of brotherhood such as pasture land and its grazing cattle, fields of grain, flowers, birds and woodland.

"But, in this apparent contradiction of opposites you will find the great depth of wisdom which underlie our philosphies and has equalized a limitation of the brain to maintain a rational balance of human characteristic under impact of an advancing science that sought to parry and survive a dying planet. My ancient forebears fully realized that unborn generations to come, conceived in this privation of adversity that may last for thousands of years and to be compressed in a world of chemistry, bounded by lifeless metallic walls of a ship, could only evolve as automatons, a race of human robots unable to know the value of love or even a contemplation, in beauty, of their origin; if, they had never seen a flower in bloom, a tree to grow, heard the song of a bird or watched the freedom of an animal's movements. The human brain is a marvel of the Universe, but it is also an extremely susceptible entity.

"And now," said Zret, like a mean old witch waving a magic wand, "we are back in a drifting canoe on the

Hudson twenty thousand years later."

"Does this end my lesson for today?" I rather disheart-
eningly asked.

"If you had your way that brain of yours would become
so cluttered as to make comprehensive evaluation impossible. Remember, I am the teacher and wish to be a good
one, so it is also necessary to determine your ability to
assimilate this teaching in knowledgeable pattern. I, for
one, am going to take a swim and after to concentrate a
little more fully on our fishing."

These meetings, the dinners and the trips are typical
of countless that grew into years and through Zret's patience, the deep sincerity of friendship and guidance of
wisdom, the tantalizing puzzle of a Universe, its population of stars and galaxies, of planets and their animals and
people slowly rounded into the understanding that he had
promised, but also endowed, a far more precious gift of
philosophy that merges love with the beauty of life and
the blessing of perfect health.

CHAPTER 6
NOTATIONS OF LATER
STUDY SESSIONS WITH
ZRET

THE TRANSMIGRATION OF SOLAR SYSTEMS

"Less than a century passed, after the experimental flight of our Norca Ship, when the fickle Summertime period of an ice age ended. With a return of its extreme cold the receding glaciers once again started to advance and although not as massive as those that built up on Earth, due to far less plentiful water distribution, they did rob a considerable amount from the shallow seas, lakes and rivers, which in many instances were completely frozen and remained in this solidified state for several hundreds of years.

"Atmospheric thinning continued to add its complications and when the permanent warming trend finally arrived, they watched their planet slowly die, for during the next five thousand years the sun evaporated an unequal percentage of water and melting ice that returned in the form of runoff and in rain and snow patterns. The people of Norca made a valiant effort, employing every scientific tool at their command, but could not retard this vapor drain off for the dehydrating atmosphere lost its ability to effectively diffuse the sun's heat radiation, resulting in an ever increasing speed up of escape electrons in air and water molecules.

"The ice caps eventually dwindled away, later followed by the remaining water of river, lake and sea. The fertile lands dried up and deteriorated to the dust, sand and stone of the relentlessly expanding great central desert. All plant life of former sea and soil withered away and without this basic source of atmospheric oxygen and food supply the animal kingdoms vanished and also vanishing with them was man's waning hope to stem the inexorable forces that strip an aging planet of its living mantle.

"Only one avenue from total extinction remained open; evacuation and the last years of habitation in a native environment was rather a frugal existence that they endured, living between their remarkable ships and the surface of this dying world as they studied, calculated and plotted a course to a contemporary solar system. This study and its evaluation were painstakingly thorough as there was little tolerable allowance for error and decision of choice restricted to the elements of velocity, time and distance, for contact with a water bearing planet.

"Velocity of the vehicles well established, in continuous flight, at thirty-eight thousand miles per second and travel distance limited by a time span of sixty-five years; the exhaustion point of chemical and water supply capacities, through their reprocessing systems, in sustaining a compliment of selected animals, plants and two hundred forty-three thousand men, women and children, the remaining representation of a once mighty nation who, through so many thousands of years of natural adversity, had been forced to counter balance a population in a strict practice of birth control.

"The star which they called Ni Runth, our sun, was situated within this time-space radius from Tau Ceti and all electronic probes confirmed that at least two of its indicated planets were water bearing and compatible to the materialization of matter in compounds from which they had evolved.

"After the electronic verification of computed calculation, a momentous decision to direct their path of flight to this solar system was unanimously acclaimed. In a touching ceremony of farewell, a brief history of their nation with date and intended destination of migration, was inscribed upon the white cliffs face that once loaned its beauty to the side of a verdant valley only now to stand stark and naked against a blazing sky, but each person filing past knelt to kiss the base of this stone in a heartbreaking gesture of good-bye to an origin of birth, then faces bathed in unabashed tears as they made their way to allotted locations in the sixty-two ships of the fleet.

"Each one of the forty passenger ships, a sister and replica of the Norca Ship, housing fifty-one hundred people and several hundred animals of the bovine, horse, sheep, antelope, dog and cat families, fifteen specie of bird-life, plus many genera of plants and insects on their scientifically engineered farms. The twenty-two transports were laid out in similar smaller pattern to compliment approximately one thousand seven hundred seventy men and women who were the technicians in charge of the major portion of all materials, machines, electronic devices, laboratory and research instruments, etc., stowed on these ships and so a determined civilization began its fantastic journey to a hoped for haven that promised the last and only salvation of their race.

"The main duration of flight, which lasted fifty-eight years and seven months, brought them to the fringe influences of our solar system and was quite uneventful, without too great a change from the mode of existence they had experienced and became accustomed to in those last years of proximity to their native planet, except an understandable apprehension regarding the ultimate goal. But with this goal in sight and their hopes keyed to the exhilaration of victory, disaster did strike, for the opposing polarities of their ships, of the electronic devices and guidance systems, that had served so well and accurately over these many millions of miles, was the apparent impetus that terminated an epic flight in a horrible holocaust."

(This miscalculation never was fully confirmed.) The sun apparently acted as a gigantic magnet and they were powerless to fully check the tremendous velocities, as their ships fell uncontrollable into its fiery mass. Three planets were in the general line of fall and at least two of the plummeting ships hit Jupiter. (Never heard of again) One crashed on Mars and another into Venus (Fragments later found.)

"Through some miracle of destiny the original experimental ship intersected the path of Mars and did not bum up, explode or shatter on impact, but ricocheted and after several decreasing orbits of this planet, skipped across the sand, dust and hummocks of its surface to finally partially bury itself in a large lull that split wide open, to only demolish the leading edge, as the most incomprehensible event of all enabled the survival of thirty-seven hundred of its occupants.

"After recovery from the shock stress that terminated this journey of hope, caring for the injured, both animal and human and cremation of the dead, repeated attempts to communicate with other craft of the fleet resulted in negative response as they prepared for tentative probes of this strange planet on which they were now marooned and at first glance did not seem much more hospitable than the homeland that they had fled. The atmosphere was quite thin, with pressure a fraction under six pounds per square inch at mean surface level, resolving in moderately temperate days and cold nights, but a widening scope of exploration revealed they had landed on one of the extensive deserts of its equatorial zone and that there was water—not overly abundant—with higher atmospheric pressure both to the North and the South, with some plant and small animal life predominated by the rodent and reptile families, a few specie of fish and millions of insects, but no trace of humanoid form.

"There were also shallow ice caps at either pole that represented a dormant reservoir to be tapped through engineering technique. The planet did not appear in an exact category of embracing extinction, but rather in the essence of marking time in an arrest from natural deterioration. The span duration that it would remain in this state could not be immediately determined, but at best, it promised no paradise.

"So ends the story of the valiant flight of my venerable ancestors as a pitiful remnant renewed a struggle to retain its grasp on a spark of life with scarcely the rudiments of existence at their command."

Farewell to the Planet of Origin

The illustration depicts the barren desolation of a planet that had died. Naked stone, dust, sand and craters, its only feature. Yet a land of origin; "Home," lives deep in the heart of all. A reluctance to leave pulls at these heart strings, even in the face of an inevitable flight of salvation. Before each contingent boards an arriving craft; they gather under an inscription on the base of a great white cliff, in sad farewell.

CHAPTER 7
THE SURVIVORS

"The first decade in this strange environment was a precarious period; their great ship lay crippled and beyond repair; yet a haven of shelter, with some of its life sustaining functions still intact; but the "transports" with their precious cargoes of much needed material, machinery, electronic devices, laboratory equipment and the personnel of these many sciences, destroyed or beyond the pale of a now curtailed communication system. Every phase of this incredible incidence was an interlinking of the irony of fate with the whimsical caprices of luck. The compliment of this ship of destiny were, in major part, scientists of the Agricultural field and its associated branches of agrology, animal husbandry, etc., with only a minor percentage of Engineers, Electronic specialists and physicists.

"But again the knowledge of this overall group of naturalists and the experience of long years of adversity, on their homeland, was the basic nucleus that overcame the hostile conditions of this unique planet.

"Centuries before, the concentrated studies of plant life and soil by this science had disclosed that the requisites of existence may be coaxed from a most barren locale and the knowledge of this exacting research once more put to good use, for it had also revealed how trees and plants live out a complete cycle, minus a nervous system, breathe without benefit of gills, lung or the presence of oxygen; circulate sap, their life blood, without a heart or other distinct pumping mechanism and the intricate method of combining electronics, hydrolysis, chemistry and energy, through which they convert lifeless, inorganic elements into the compound foods that are the basic sustenance of all involving animate forms. They had also originated complex compounds, derived from insect and bacteriological sources, that contained tremendous protein and mineral value when used as a food supplement.

"Our Educational Curriculum has always comprised an elementary term of twenty-one years, in which all of our known sciences are studied and a final five year term or major, in the science that the student has shown a more comprehensive adaptitude during the elementary term. With this general knowledge of their earlier schooling, a scanty population was welded into a previous national structure of fifty-six sciences as they endeavored to recapture a way of life under philosophies of love and beauty.

"It was just over a thousand years later than these scientists of a growing nation, had unraveled the mysteries of this solar systems magnetic fields, its energy potential and velocity power sources. They then proceeded to design and construct the ships that were used to harness this power, as they launched twin expeditions of exploration to the neighboring planets of Venus and Earth. The success of these missions would guarantee a security to life if their planet became untenantable and to perhaps fulfill a dream in their unrelenting search for a more compatible environment in which to expand their studies and to fully enjoy the benefit that this knowledge and its application in a refinement of nature may bestow."

(Author's note.) At this point of the story I feel the necessity of inserting an excerpt, from the fourth letter of the series of six, which these "Modern Technicians from Space" have dispatched during the past 11 years. It not only gives insight as to the tremendous wealth of history, knowledge and philosophy which these letters contain, but the text of this specific excerpt as translated and adapted to our understanding, by these strangers, is taken from the ancient archives and flight log of this original exploration of our planet more than thirteen thousand years ago. I believe that this passage, written in the words of these intrepid explorers, is far more impressive than any that I may coin.

Excerpt from their letter dated May 31, 1962

"The following narrative is taken from our records and as space requisites of a letter, limit complete elucidation and detail, an epitome of generalities will be employed in a succession of occurring events and in the main, in present tense, as a picture unfolding. Familiar terms will be used.

"We have come to the conclusion that our planet is slowly dying and although there is no imminent danger, we do know that at some point, in the foreseeable millenniums of the future, it will become incapable of sustaining life if allowed to deteriorate in its natural cycle and in consequence are working on four tremendous projects."

1 A method to nudge the planet a little closer to the sun, this a questionable undertaking for the calculated effect that an unnatural motion of this mass, in a third directional velocity, may have on it and on neighboring planets is difficult to determine, with the possibility of upsetting the very delicate balance of opposing force which constitutes the life and behavior of all planets.

2 A method of temperature moderation.

3 A method of increasing water supply.

4 A craft for interplanetary travel with the verification of a great deal of our calculation dependent on physical check through this project and also a guarantee of survival should conditions ever warrant a mass evacuation.

"The basis of this narrative will concern a part of the latter project and its initial objective: the exploration of the twin planets, Earth and Venus, which for so many years have been studied through visual observation. At last this great moment has arrived, several reconnaissance flights have been completed, tests made for radiation of the atmosphere and a general evaluation of the environment which we may encounter, for life on both planets appear to be primitive as there is no visible evidence of cities or other form and order which indicate civilized man.

"Two expeditions are ready for takeoff, each with a separate objective, but of the same intent, the landing for scientific research on alien planets. Our paraphernalia has been stowed with many bundles of food, clothing, utensils, implements and ornaments to be used, as gifts, should we meet fellow man. So our journey begins - fifteen men and their wives winging into a vast unknown, for all except the four who had blazed the test flight trails with the hope and the dreams of our people ever with us, a great joy fills the hearts of all in a pride of achievement—our destination the blue tinted sphere. Earth—the insignia on our banner, Anna, a star.

"For four hundred and ninety-seven hours we voyage as the awe inspiring panorama of our solar system unfolds, but ever blending with the unfathomable mysteries of the universe whose stars dazzle, bewitch and lure as the hidden fire of diamonds in this black velvet setting, the blazing sun is our constant companion, the dot on our scanners increasing as each hour flies by until we hover over a shimmering jewel of fleecy clouds, sparkling water and green vegetation.

"We drop lower, the earth pattern with landlocked seas, lakes and rivers stand out, mountains take shape, some indicate volcanic action, great soil rooted forests become distinguishable from fern and swamp vegetation as we make several circles of the planet in general observation. In many of the open areas we note manlike figures scurrying for cover and at each, we drop a few of our gift bundles. After this close scrutiny and study of the terrain we confirm that life is in a primitive stage and prepare for our initial landing. Excitement is running high, for we are approaching the spot which we had previously chosen for this unprecedented event, a plateau, nestled in a valley of pine, palm and cypress.

"It is situated approximately due west of the Cape Verde Islands on a large stretch of land which reaches from below the tip of present Africa to within six hundred miles of Greenland. We drop to a few feet above ground and pause for several minutes. Nothing stirs, all is silence except for the rustling of the palm fronds in the breeze. We settle slowly and rest solidly on Earth and for about a half an hour just watch. Then came the twittering and song of the birds, the first living sounds of a new world, our hatches slide open and the warm, heavy, humid air filters into the ship but we do not experience too much difficulty in breathing, the access ramps slip silently to the ground and we emerge to a land of breathtaking wonder, an overwhelming emotion of joy, of thankfulness brings tears to the eyes of all but even they cannot dim the perceptive beauty of the flora, the bright plumage of the birds, the blue haze hanging in the mountains of this wonderland.

"We transmit news of success back home and plant our banner, a white flag with its bright blue star, which for almost two hundred years was to be a symbolization of love, advancement and achievement in this new world.

"After the first joyous, emotional surge we took stock of the surroundings, made tests of the water, soil, stone, plant and trees. Classified many types of insect, lizards, snakes, fish, and birds, the snakes being the larger of the animals that we encountered the first day. We also noted that the gift bundles, which we dropped previously, had not been touched but lay as they had fallen. In our period of observation we had seen many large campfires during the nights and as evening approached elected to build one in hope that it may induce the natives to come to us but we later learned they moved very little after dark and that the fires were basic procedure to ward off evil spirits and prowling animals.

"Early the next morning our instruments indicated many people around the ship and we could see movement amid the trees so decided to have breakfast, in the open. We kindled four small fires, opened the gift bundles and removed utensils and food. Every motion, each action very precise, very obvious and made a great show at cooking breakfast, but still they did not make an appearance.

"We had just about given up hope when we noticed a motion of the bushes, at the edge of the clearing and six children stepped into view. They came forward slowly, hesitantly, with several backward glances. We did not move but continued eating as they approached to within a few feet of our circle and stopped. Six small, light blue skinned female children with brown eyes and straight black hair. All were naked and although they were very cautious, seemed a bit more curious than frightened, as a little flock of birds but ready to take wing at the first sign of danger.

"One of the girls reached behind her with a platter of cakes, made patty style, of cornmeal and crystallized honey and motioned for them to eat but they would not budge, so it was set on the ground and as she moved away they pounced on it and darted back to the woods. We cleaned up the remainder of breakfast, washed and put the utensils away, opened the other bundles and beckoned for them to come.

"At last curiosity must have overcome their fear for one hundred and thirty men, women and children came out of the woods, all were blue skinned and scantily clad. The men carried clubs, stone axes and stone tipped spears and ranged between six feet six inches to seven feet in height with well proportioned bodies. At they came to within about fifty feet of us, the weapons were grasped in both hands and stretched crossways over their heads, this we took for a gesture of friendship so held up bright colored cloth, ribbons, necklaces and types of adz and axes from the bundles in the same manner and the response was instantaneous for they came on the run, laughing and whooping like children.

"We opened containers of juice, dried, candied and preserved fruit and vegetables, cakes, a type of bread and smoked fish. It was a great day of joy, our girls draped the cloth, garment fashion, on the women, fixed ribbons in their hair, adorned them with bracelets and necklaces. They were especially intrigued with the sandals, many of which were worked with a silver like filigree and colored stones. We demonstrated the use of the knife, the axe, the fishhook and the net.

"We had many implements of cultivation but were a little beyond their comprehension and our music held them spellbound. They were extremely friendly and appreciative of our interest in their well-being and during the next two weeks we accompanied the men on several trips of exploration.

"We encountered the boar and water-buffalo, the rhinoceros, hippopotamus, crocodile and the jaguar, leopard and tiger like cats, the antelope and the great elephant to mention a few. We developed quite a sign language and learned many of their words, phrases and habits. They were basically nomads and lived from the land, the villages consisting of temporary shelters of poles, grass and palm thatch and they traveled in bands, more akin to herds, for there was no basic code of law, merely the rule of right by might, just as the more powerful bull of the animal led his herd.

"There was no religion but they lived in constant fear of spirits and everything had a spirit, with very little differential between living and dead, manifest and hallucination for they blended until they became synonymous and a terrifying reality as darkness fell. Due to negative thinking their sleep was plagued with dreams and nightmares. The swift lunge of the animal, the hiss of the snake, the howling winds and storms, falling trees and rocks to crush them and the agonizing screams of dying comrades filled their nights. They actually gave more credence to the so-called spirit, than to reality, for the objective was something with which they could cope.

"Their dead were carefully wrapped in a matting of grass, palm fronds and mud and placed in special caves. We learned that they had no realistic comprehension of death for the spirit of a friend or relative accompanied them on the hunt, in battle and often visited at night.

"They held our craft in awe and wonder and each time they passed would touch it, as though it were a special pet or friend, we tried to explain that we had come from one of the stars in the sky and this completely mystified them but they did consider us all the good spirits rolled into one. It came time to move on and they were very reluctant for us to leave, but we told them to guard our banner well and to watch the sky for we would return with many of our people to teach and to free them from fear, strife, and want. We made many stops during the next two months and charted a good deal of your planet.

"On several occasions the natives were hostile but we merely stunned them and removed their weapons and when they came to, fed them, in this way gained their confidence, for they were always hungry. We also created a great deal of good will from our bright colored cloth and ornaments, for it never failed to fascinate. One comical aspect developed from the pots and pans and some containers which we had dropped in our gift bundles, for upon landing at these sites, we found many of the men wearing them as helmets.

"We classified the natives in five major groups, according to skin pigmentation. The golden race (by far the more numerous) inhabiting the land of east southern Europe, across Asia and Lemuria almost to the shores of central America. The white race in Greenland, across northern and central Europe and Asia to Siberia. The copper race from Siberia to the tip of South America. The blue race in central and northern Atlantis and across north central Africa. The black race, southern Atlantis and Africa to Borneo. The races had one characteristic in common, all had black hair and their eyes varied from light brown to black.

"After completing two and one-half months of adventure and research we returned home, our craft loaded with specimens of soil, mineral, plant, insect and some animal life and to assist in the planning for colonization of this new land.

"Our first city, which later developed into the greater of all, was established at the site of our initial landing, the second in Peru, the third at a point which would be just east of the Marshall Islands, the next in southern Tibet and the last in Lebanon. From these five great centers we began to fan our colonies. We had very little trouble with the natives; in fact they were all eagerly awaiting our coming and willing to work with us and very anxious to learn. In the beginning our one great problem was their warlike and belligerent attitude toward each other, for they knew of only one way to settle disputes, might and brute force, no matter how trivial the differences.

"Our first established laws were codes of retaliation, a hurt for a hurt, a burn for a burn and so on and demonstrated that might was not right for a child with a lever could move a stone that the most powerful man could not budge, a weaker man with a small device, could cut a rock in half or as easily disintegrate a herd of elephants and that the only asset of brute strength was in physical prowess of the athlete in competitive games for enjoyment and not as a basis in a pattern of living. These codes were later softened by those of cause and effect and of arbitration.

"One of the first simple examples of explanation, in the working of these laws, illustrated in the fact that if a branch of a fruit tree fell and caused injury or death to a person, that it was not a willful deed and that to destroy the tree for this unpremeditated act would also deprive man of the benefit of its fruit, which he would enjoy for many years. Killing in any manner was absolutely forbidden with a penalty of banishment forever to a remote and inaccessible part of the land.

"The only penalties invoked for disobedience to and the breaking of the rules was to rescind the right to work, the participation in social activities or banishment to the forest to forage for themselves for periods of time in respect to the severity of the infraction. In twenty years, through patience, tolerance and a philosophy founded on the beauty of thought and of love and in the education of the children in these principles we had developed five intelligent and culturally advanced communities.

"They had learned to cultivate the land and the rudiments of animal husbandry for we had introduced cotton, corn, wheat, barley, beans, yams, potatoes, apples and plums. The horse, the dairy cow, sheep, the greyhound and house cat and they were also becoming adept in many of the arts and crafts. As security replaced want and negative thinking their fear of spirits gradually disappeared.

"We colonized on the basis of equality to all with no distinction as to race or color and our only superiority that of teachers and guides in a new way of life. (Your white race has always been the more aggressive and giving a subtle feeling of contemptuous tolerance in their dealings with others.)

"As the years passed into a century we had established many cities, universities, centers of research and arenas for racing, sport and games. Treachery was not in our minds but a few incidents did occur during the next forty years, which should have put us on guard. The first came in the form of resentment to our private centers, used for visitors and councils from the motherland. Viciousness often invaded the competitive games, an apparent stray arrow would find its mark in one of our people, at an archery contest.

"Many of our scientists researching metal, propulsion, rays and electronics preferred to work in seclusion and this request had always been honored by our people but not so with your ancestors, for they felt that they were being barred although they had access to every principle but one, and were working on a majority of projects with our scientists. The one principle, which was not divulged, the breakdown of the atomic structure of matter and it had been a closely guarded secret since its development, for although its benefits were many it also had a potential force to destroy, even to a planet, if used unwisely.

101

"During the next few years agitation arose from these and other imagined grievances, societies were formed from which we were banned and rumors were spreading as to our foreign status, invaders from another land. In the past we had adopted a magnanimous attitude toward the little differences, petty jealousies and flare-ups, did not realize that the urge of nationalism, the lust for conquest had not been erased but merely lay dormant in their emotional character.

"Now they were well educated, versed in the sciences, engineering, the arts and crafts, had their elected leaders and ruling councils who apparently decided that we had outlived our usefulness. We could no longer ignore these rumors, the veiled threats and incidents so an investigating committee was organized to determine the extent of their plan, the ultimate aim and the intended method to achieve its conclusion. A good portion of the populace was still loyal and we soon uncovered the operational strategy of its scheme.

"A plan of staggering magnitude, for we had been completely unaware of the theft of the formula of disintegration by means of a trick of light refraction and was being used to fashion devices of destruction and conquest. It figured that our annihilation here would be the initial phase of the campaign and then on to the other planets.

"We gathered as many of our women and children as the available craft would carry and sent them home and flashed an S O S for help and equipment. We made hasty attempt, with the limited facilities at hand, to devise a neutralizing system but did not know exactly where or to what extent they had succeeded in their buildup and our help never had time to arrive for they apparently panicked through the knowledge of our discovery of this insidious plot.

"Through haste, error in construction design or lack of preconceived method of control, the world literally came to an end. The main concentration of power was directed at our centers of Atlantis and Lemuria, by far the larger and most graceful of all our artistic creation in this new world. Enchanted cities and communities of wondrous beauty, conceived in love and built for the joy, the comfort and expediency of all. A cultural excellence which has never again been equalled.

"The energy force waves traveled from north to south, swelling as they advanced, everything in its path turned to dust and disappeared, the natural land barriers disintegrated and the seas swept in, causing tremendous earthquakes and volcanic action, entire continents exploded and were hurled into space.

"The earth's orbital velocity quickened and it skidded off on a slight tangent but stabilized a million miles further from the sun and although its rotation did not cease, a new wobble added to the devastation and the turbulence did not exhaust itself for many years. Approximately two thirds of the planet was sheathed in ice. The greatest miracle of all was that a small percentage of life did, somehow, manage to survive.

"For more than three thousand years the planet lie, as though dead, the only sign of life was isolated splotches of green vegetation but the seed seems indestructible. Plant and tree followed the recession of the ice, in the deeply frozen areas the remnants of animal and human life multiplied and man again emerged with his warlike traits in tribal form. Many were integrated collections of several races for their fight for survival had been fraught with hardship and adversity.

"We had decreed to leave this world of human beasts strictly on its own and to hope that at some time the blood of our own people, which now ran in the veins of some, would eventually predominate. Over the centuries we have made periodic checks, just to see how things were going and have left observers to record the evolution of the intelligent idiot.

"A vision of paradise and the horrible catastrophe which ended it never left the minds of the people and although we did not have the opportunity to benefit the majority, before the holocaust most had the knowledge of us and awaited our coming. As time dimmed memory, actuality, to these remnants of races was replaced with myth and legend but forever after have they turned to the sky, in supplication for aid from the stress of need and despair.

Initial Observation of Man of Planet Earth

The observation period before landing and exploration of Earth, 13,000 years ago, by Zret's ancestors. The men pictured are "Cro-Magnon" the last of our primitive white forbears. They roamed parts of the planet, more in the essence of animal herds, than in a social science of civilization. It was about 100 years later that "Modern Man" came into almost immediate essential being, without the long transition of evolution; but through education and intermarriage with this race from outer space.

Initial Contact with Earth's Races

The first touchdown for exploration of Earth was in north central "Atlantis." A now fabled land on which the elemental human being of Earth originated, 16 million years ago. Here were slowly evolved the present Negro races and the practically extinct Blue race. The Negro was the first branch off of ancestral primate stock to achieve primal Human Status. His evolution began in southern Atlantis. The Blue race, next in line, evolved in northern Atlantis. Six little female children of the Blue race were the first contactees with these explorers from Outer Space.

When the Human Brain Conceived Its First Destructive Device

An innocent device of benefit was researched for its power to destroy by the white race of Earth, who had been educated and raised to a high state of intelligence by Zret's ancestors. In a parallel of today, the descendants of this same white race have researched the Atom, the creative power of a Universe, to reveal its secrets for slaughter and conquest through military might. Just 12,800 years ago "The Vehicle" of this first research was turned loose. Land barriers deteriorated, billions of tons of sea water instantly vaporized, to release the sodium content of its salt that had been stabilized in solution, tremendous explosion, earthquake and volcanic reaction drowned out the screams of the dying as a continent exploded. The ocean finally inundated the scene of this holocaust and today roll placidly over a graveyard of horror that was once a land of life and beauty. The first attempt at unleashing natures' latent destructive power, as a tool of mans lust, ended in shattering a portion of a planet's face. Who may foretell the result of a next attempt?

CHAPTER 8
A VOLUNTARY
MISSION

Planet Earth has circled its sun some twelve thousand, eight hundred times since this first humanly conceived device triggered an uncontrollable phase of nature's own latent potential of self-destruction that shattered its face. This rhythmic passage of time has healed most of its wounds, as it too advances a story to the dawn of the twentieth century.

Our calendar year was 1901 when, twenty-six million miles distant, "Zret" and many of his colleagues were gathered in a conference hall to discuss an issue of vital importance with their governing council, an eminent body comprising twenty-eight men and twenty-eight women, each an elected representative of the fifty-six sciences. The topic of concentrated interest was this same earth and its modern inhabitants.

The review of gathered fact definitely emphasized that our era of man power, the horse, windpower and hand to hand combat was rapidly drawing to a close. A budding science had powered ships, locomotives and industry; in part, with steam. The combustion engine and electrical energy were coming into their own. Plans and experimentation on heavier than air flying machines were in the process of eventual test flight and scientific probes were scratching the surface of nuclear physics. In 1895, the X-ray was discovered; a year later, radio activity and in 1897, an initial step toward the Atom as the English physicists J. J. Thomson uncovered negative particles, which he named "corpuscles" and claimed were an integral part of universal materialization; but they knew that the "electron" had been isolated and ever combining with each new discovery; new invention, every war was becoming a little more deadly than its proceeding counterpart.

The great question mark of these considerations was "gunpowder", the standard medium to military manipulation and its destructive power, yet, quite harmless to foment a planetary catastrophe. The crux of determination was the span of years that it may retain this status before it also was relegated to the use of origin, a firecracker. Unanswerable questions and a dilemma arose as to which path we would pursue, what counteractive to become necessary if a refinement and expansion of this art of slaughter was abetted by scientific research.

Conjecture and argument centered on four alternatives of replacement; chemistry and gas, electronic rays, sonic disintegration and their graver concern, nuclear fission/fusion. Which would predominate? Or would the scientists of various major countries dabble in all four, prodded relentlessly on by their governments in a quest of military supremacy? In this event all divergent paths must inevitably converge to create the super potential of an exploding planet and the remote—but not in the realm of impossibilities—breakdown of a stabilized sun.

Definitions of solution resolved in one unanimous conclusion: intimate contact with the people of Earth through a cryptic infiltration into specific families of engineers and physicists.

Study with them, work with them, as one of their own and in this way have their fingers on the pulse of trend. Any spectacular breakthrough could then be immediately evaluated and if it embodies a tendency to cataclysmic reaction, procedure in fundamentals of a neutralizer be worked out in secrecy as the device was developed.

Once this pattern of thought was established, deliberation was centered on formulation, ruling and the selection of personnel.

The entire undertaking was instituted as a system of honor, on a voluntary basis, with the maximum period of participation fixed at one hundred years, a necessary time limitation for their return to undergo the rejuvenescent process that was indispensable to the extension of life expectancy. In the beginning quite a controversy developed with the female element through their desire to volunteer for this worthy mission; but after explanation and decision by the council they were convinced of the impracticability of exposure to the unfamiliar and barbaric practices of Earth.

In some countries a woman was a mere chattel in the household. The horror endured by womanhood under the conquering armies of warfare and even in highly cultured countries, they may be subjected to the humiliation of beatings; molestation; rape and perhaps death; from lust or crime and that the male physique would eliminate many of these unpredictable potentials.

As the plan rounded into a course of action, specialists were sent to Earth to scout three hundred fifty families for computation and synchronization of the intricate details in this complex program and its coordination with their home laboratories. This study was accomplished in two years and the one hundred volunteers carried to the designated cities of every major country on Earth during the months from February to June of 1904 in an unprecedented method to infiltrate a nucleus that may anticipate and forestall any future debacle resulting from the misdirected genius of the human brain.

Complete freedom of action by these one hundred technicians was limited by a set of five inviolate rulings and subtitles for the duration of their stay on Earth. Any infraction to these rules would subject the violator to immediate recall and if unforeseen events necessitated an amendment to procedure only a majority vote by the council could rescind or change its stipulations.

The following is a general transcript of its basic embodiment:

1. Secrecy of identity was paramount. Intervention or instigation of any change in our way of life was strictly forbidden.

2. To willfully participate in armed conflict; to divulge any secret of physics or chemistry that may even remotely aid in an expansion of military potential; or to direct or assist in the planning of a military strategy was also forbidden.

3. No man of Earth was permitted entrance to a space craft.

4. Due to possibility of a maximum duration of this mission, marriage with Earth women was permitted; but a specific element, in the chemistry of the body was electronically treated to prevent the occurrence of offspring. Permanent roots would not be tolerated.

5. To always conduct themselves as gentlemen and the mannerisms, thought, kindness and tolerance of their own philosophies be extended in all dealings with our people and to assist in any invention or philosophy of our own creation that may bring a benefit of happiness to the races of Earth.

At first their attitude was one of reserve, under impression they had come to evaluate the actions of a strange race of belligerent, semi-animalistic humans whose ferocity in the art of warfare may ultimately lead to self destruction; but as they readapted to our mode of existence and in the love of their adopted mothers, later marriage and a widening circle of friendships; they recognized the many redeeming qualities that seemed to lay dormant or smothered by the unrealistic doctrines of our social science.

They were also conscious of the fact that these fallacies; so vividly pinpointed in their eyes through a status of outsiders looking in, were our normal and accepted way of life, even to certain justification of armed conflict and completely unaware that a higher station of culture could only be attained if wisdom divorced regimentation by brute force from our philosophies.

Documentation of this appraisal was sent to their council with feelers for a conditional softening of the stipulations under which they were bound; but, once again, they were cautioned against interference in our economic or social systems which could only suffer by comparison and any benefit nullified by its chaos of confusion.

A true refinement of doctrine could only be accomplished by the combining efforts of our theological, scientific and governmental leaders in a slow transition of merging social understanding and the research of factual science into compatible appreciation of universal motivation. The very gesture of attempting to interfere may also put the entire mission in jeopardy if its intent and their true identities were revealed. So, over the years, their unobtrusive influence, although never apparent, can be found in many of the boons which have given us a little boost above the drudgery of the past.

By 1939 they were fully aware that our scientific endeavor was in the initial stages of exploiting the atom for nuclear destruction and concentrated their energies on method and fabrication of a neutralizing screen to counteract a hydrogen chain reaction; that would insure the integral mass of Planet Earth should the massed genius of its human brain unleash an uncontrollable force through an under estimation of this power in phases of experimental testing or in the madness of warfare.

But a desire to help was very strong in these one hundred who have lived with our races over this period of time and their unceasing efforts finally achieved a leniency which has enabled the limited contacts and attempt at debate after the screen was energized in 1958 and a subsequent series of letters. These letters covered many subjects and some characterized in forceful review the utter disregard of life and lack of human compassion as armies and empires have rolled over the bones of the weaker and less fortunate in a history of conquest.

Just prior to completion of this book, I have appeared on several radio broadcasts and the story's general outline publicized in a series of newspaper articles with mixed reaction, but in overall enthusiastic reception. Of course, in some instances, I have been classified as a nut and in the opinion of one commentator, under the influence of a con man for forty-seven years. An eminent scientist considered the book as scientific mumbo-jumbo, designed to confuse; but their memories appear to be very short as they forget that a few years ago they would have been categorized in the realm of the unbalanced and perhaps their findings condemned as works of the devil.

Although we are now in the process of merely scratching the surface of universal motivation, there is a tendency in the human brain to bog down in a smugness of contemporary conviction and anything foreign to this assumed apex of status- quo viewed with the greatest of skepticism.

This closing chapter will carry excerpts from the last

letter in a series of six which these strangers have dispatched and as our own advancing research delves ever deeper in scientific study of geology, paleontology, the electronic spectrum and mysterious reaches of space. It will definitely confirm if this knowledge is only scientific mumbo-jumbo, designed to confuse, or whether a vastly superior intelligence did attempt to sow the seeds that may clarify and become the slender guideline of thought; to create a far greater happiness and security, than we have ever before experienced.

- Excerpts from letter #6 -
January 10, 1965
The Earth, In General.
Gentlemen,

Previous letters, in essence, have been an analytic criticism of demographic law that has muddled through the pages of time, unable to separate fact from fancy and to dramatize the acts of ego and the arrogance of ideology which refuses to establish the relative balance of matter to matter. As fancy becomes a shaping force in a way of life it must inevitably, consummate in a chaos of thought and the social science complied from the prophecies of this neo-primitive dogma, combining a limited understanding of observable environment with the fiction of forces wholly undetermined, cannot but hang, endlessly, in a vacuum of suspension as internal conflict forbids stabilization.

These tenets, welling from the untrained, the unscientific mind, have merely distorted, for examination of this Cosmological Problem through the unbiased scrutiny of science, reveals an immeasurable cauldron of uncontrolled force, of turbulence. It is brewed in the violence of parasitical motivation and patterned in geometric lines of creation, destruction, rebirth; through exothermic and endothermic action of energy - but - absolutely devoid of love and compassion.

This minus factor in animalistic association and environmental adaptitude, can and must be applied by present, more highly evolved atomic creation in the materialization of man. But, if he stumbles onward, eyes blinded in egoism and superstitious fear, his laws only abet these awesome forces, rather than bend them to a will, in a determination of equalizing philosophy.

- Excerpt #2 from letter #6 -

Creations, by trial and error, march in endless review as various peculiarities of form have, for fleeting moments and by brute forces, dominated a specific time locale of Earth. Most have not survived, as completed entities, many being destroyed by catastrophe and still others have succumbed to diversification environment and climate, as we move slowly up to the present, more highly evolved, mental specimen in the structure of Homo Sapien. His ultimate station in life and sad, but so very true, all other matter form, in close proximity to his habitat, are governed by the wisdom applied in the justice of this criteria with the possible exception of the minute and microscopic kingdoms which, at times, play so much hob with the body, of this superior mind.

But, does he actually derive his true fill of benefit, from this exalted position? He sits astride a pinnacle of self inflation, lacking the deep meditation necessary to mitigation of forces which are the base of his composite as a wonderful brain is wasted in the conception of larger and more hideous weapons and method to annihilate not only his specie but to denude the atmosphere, the lands and the waters of all other kingdoms, through thoughtless application. Will you, too, slip into the oblivion of yesterdays, as Intelligence fails to surmount this rigid law of Adversity in a fate shared by all brute dominated eras of the past?

You look, askance at all other creation as inferior, yet, can a difference be discerned in primal thought reaction between two opposing Ant Armies, locked in mortal combat as their powerful mandibles tear each other to shreds and the Human Soldier, with flame thrower in hand and an array of high explosives as he slaughters a so-called Enemy? Unreservedly, in this instance, our vote of confidence must go to the Ant for, at least, he is not attempting the destruction of an environment or the poisoning of an atmosphere, in which the ultimate survivor may hope to exist.

- Excerpt #3 from letter #6 -

Varying materialization of "Hominidae" have roamed the surface crust of this planet for many millions of years, yet, except for one fleeting moment a workable insight as to constitution six miles below the feet or to its ocean bottoms almost as hazy today as when the first seedlings of land life crawled from the haven of its depths into the brilliant sun of a distant past. Thorough research of these unexplored domains, will give rise to sobering implications regarding geology and life form patterns.

Also, throughout this period, you have traveled uncountable billions of miles with your planet in the effortless ease of a magnetic line of force, but regardless, without confirmation and only elemental research as to inner mechanism and safeguards you plan to leave this surface and explore a vast dimension within the weightless confines of an artificially propelled projectile, in defiance to all characteristic of evolved environment. Yes, earthman is in possession of superior intellect but its application surely manifests in peculiar practice and many weird customs.

During the past seventy years, through improved instrumentation in basic research, glimmerings of truth have been defined but, to date, cannot seem to establish a conformity to the benefit which this new found knowledge presents. We have followed the probing of your eminent philosophers and physicists in their effort to extract logic from the negation of theory that surrounds a great truth and have felt with them the vexation that the fear of ostracism, not only from the "power" organizations but that which the ignorance of social prejudice have created and until very recently an almost insurmountable obstacle in the supplanting of mysticism with factual science.

But a few have had the power of conviction and the courage to break precedent. Although advance has been agonizingly slow and in full comprehension of the paradox we can well understand their dilemma as to the interjection of research proof, into a fantasy of hierarchy. Of this eminent group one man stands without peer in the personage of Albert Einstein and surely his demise, a regrettable event in modern history and if perchance you outlive the present bomb craze, the influence of this remarkable work should carry you far along the road in a quest of understanding. Many problems he did not have time to complete and the motivation of the cosmos more or less the "will-of-the-wisp" of this research, although he came so very close to unraveling its basis of secrecy.

His principles of relativity are excellent and practicable. He discarded the Euclidian plane in favor of Geodesic conformity of Galactic cluster within a one time and three space dimensional structure, united in a specific equation of relativity and in his theory of a "Cosmological Constant" came upon the core of the riddle. We have long puzzled as to reason for abandoning this idea as his greatest mistake when all mathematical and especially his now-world famous equation point to this one and only conclusion. We often wonder if he feared the tremendous impact of truth on the earth's social structure. Yet, his model of the universe, in shape of a hypersphere, was a bit distorted, although the Principle of Equivalence, in the force fields of motion, are basic.

His apparent great dilemma arose in the question: are these fields created by motion of a space-time structure that exists independently of matter, or is the space-time structure the result of matter? He seemed unable to put his finger on the "Nucleus." This one problem has created many controversial theories with other great physicists, as expressed in the works of Newton, Mach and Sciama, Lamaiture, Gamow and of Bondi, Gold and Hoyle, to mention a recent few, under supposition of expanding and contracting universe, of the big bang or steady state, but, for the answer, we must examine this "Nucleus" and our little friend, the "Atom," for the action of galaxies is as incidental to the "Nucleus," as the "Suns" to the galaxies and the planets to the Suns and these to the "Atom," for the laws of Nature are invariant.

In the "Atom" you have discovered its electron, proton, neutron, mesons, neutrinos and many of the complexities leading up to synthesis, magnetism and motion and as Einstein would simply state, all relative to a given frame of reference. If you were to magnify this conglomeration to equivocal time-space dimension what would you have? Yes, the outline of a material universe is patterned in similarity to its creator and as you are now dissecting this microcosm, we, too, are working in parallel research with the incalculable time and expanse of the macrocosm.

Ours, an incomplete with the Universe; as yours with the atom, but the fundamentals are prime factors of a foreseeable whole.

We have discovered the "Nucleus" to be a core of pure energy at absolute Zero and devoid of Light, nor can it be penetrated, for complete decomposition results in entrance to this true Electromagnetic vehicle, resulting from a force field of motion. Its energy radiates in writhing, curling, concentric circling waves, in Magnetic lines of force and within their grip spin the galaxies, their suns, planets and elements in ceaseless motion. Galactic formation and nourishment depend entirely on this source of elemental conception although sun collision and explosion take place as do galactic interpenetration and collision, but the reconstitution of this debris within a galaxy comprises only a fraction of its structure. If it were not for this continuous outpouring from the nucleus of dynamic energy force and the unchanging pattern of higher energy components forever giving up energy to lower energy components, the abstraction of Entropy and your scientists theory of Universal Chaos would have long ago become a stark reality.

This vexing characteristic of decomposition still defies our instrumentation for mathematical computation of its inner mechanisms, or to its immensity, but combining a spectrographic analysis of galactic conformity with the partial outline of the Nucleus on impulse graphs, when carried out in the symmetry of nature, defines a slightly flattened, egg shaped sphere, with the narrow end in the direction that the galaxies are moving. What lies on the other side is as much a mystery, as the dark side of the moon to you, but you must assume that it maintains this symmetry regardless; that its complete bulk or shape has not been established.

Our probe reaches out some 15,000 million light years where we come to the turn and this bend is quite sharp. At approximately 9,000 million light years, the magnetic lines of force tend to narrow, causing a converging or closer bunching of galactic cluster, onward to the turn and at this point, all Light, Material emission and Signal ends as it melts into the impulse outline of the "Nucleus" and they disappear.

- Excerpt #4 from letter #6 -

To illustrate the many influences exerted on planetary habit and its denizens relative to various phases of galactic cycle, its position and warp inclination, we will examine the eras leading up to and embracing, the last two extremes of high noon episode, (Major glaciation periods,) which took place in your terminology of the Permeo-Carboniferous through the Pleistocene. Although events entail spans of millions of years, we will generalize on main influence in uniform continuity for the myriad variations of geology, weather, plant and animal orders would comprise volumes.

- Excerpt #5 from letter #6 -

Nearing the close of the Carboniferous Period, the warp was starting to bend on an inward plane and a foreboding of things to come the planets crust wrinkled in many areas, temperatures declined and approximately four million years, prior to the end of the Period and as our locale in the galaxy was within seven degrees of its High Noon position, relative to the Nucleus, the warps magnetic lines of force assumed a very sharp concave pattern with disastrous consequence to the solar system.

The universal grip and pull of the Nucleus, abetted by intensified centripetal reaction, causing this deep concave warp, resulted in the complete loss of our ninth planet that had its orbit between Uranus and Neptune and the destruction of the fifth, orbiting between Mars and Jupiter, for when it positioned in direct line ratio to Jupiter and the Nucleus at High Noon, it was drawn to Jupiter and pulverized. The present Asteroid Belt comprises a portion of its smaller fragments. Six Jupiter moons, as are several, orbiting the outer planets part of its pieces. The Planet that you term, Pluto, is a larger fragment and was held captive by Neptune for over 200 million years. During this cataclysm, the earth's axis shifted eighty degrees and land masses split, tremendous mountain ranges built up and ice covered sixty-seven percent of its surface for more than six million years as adversity swallowed most of its living organisms.

- Excerpt #6 from letter #6 -

As we approached High Noon and our date with the extreme forces of the "Nucleus, an outward warp held firm and as a result, the orogenesis and major glaciation period of the Pleistocene did not attain the duration or the destructive proportion of this preceding counterpart. Although many specie of animal and reptile declined and some were lost, a portion of major plant, animal and reptile groupings did survive with the only significant events on earth an inversion of its magnetic field on several occasions a few minor land breakoffs and in the solar system, Pluto was torn from Neptune's exclusive grip, but the Nucleus did not develop enough pull strength to overcome the combined hold of the Sun and Neptune in attaining a hyperbolic velocity for Pluto and it stabilized on its now erratic orbit influenced not only by the Sun and Neptune, but two now vacant warps, one between Uranus and Neptune and the other beyond that of Neptune.

Our search reveals many peculiar trends in the various time periods of galactic cycle and in a very broad sense appears as a great game of rivalry between the creative ability of the "Atom" and the nullifying forces of the Nucleus, resulting in a transient existence of all materialization and the very limited life span of most plant and animal specie groupings in their respective time elements on specific planets and once a fully developed specie declines from its evolutionary peak to a state of extinction never again to reappear naturally on a given planet.

This overall extermination and subsequent evolutionary impetus is strongly influenced by the diversification of three dominant forces: Water, Land upheaval and Temperature extreme as the reactive impact of the Nucleus in mountain building, combines with the sun in temperature variation that either rob the waters of land and sea through ice formation and evaporation or return it, by melting ice and storm tracks, in alternating cycle. The inroads of predation on the one and renascence, by interaction of sexual reproduction on the other, playing only minor roles.

It is problematical whether or not Man will dominate the remaining fifty odd million years of this afternoon, for to date, not one outstanding land animal specie has achieved this distinction, either through the entirety of a relative Morning or of an Afternoon instance; for predominance of survival spans only about ten percent or from five to six million years of these eras as they inevitably revert to testing periods in which the Atom reconstitutes, evolves and refines, in search of hardier materialization with each newer grouping a bit superior to preceding specie resulting in the present evolution of the Higher Mammal, a few Marsupials, the apparently indestructible Turtle, Shark, etc., some plant and a scattering of Synapsid and the Diapsid far distant cousins that managed to squeak through the last ordeal with the Major Nucleus forces.

Yet, Man of Planet Earth, having endured this incubus of natural calamity now poses a great question mark in the potential of his own destructive force, for this relative Afternoon had hardly begun, glacial ice was receding normally and life rising to a station it had never before achieved when adversity and greed shattered the planet, great ice sheets returned instantaneously and in the shambles of runaway natural energy, remnants of organic matter were very lucky to escape complete obliteration.

Still, if perchance, through an intelligent application

of science, Man does prove to be this durable material-ization and survives until the Night, he, as have other major specie of the past to enter this long, mild Era, will completely dominate its entirety for institution and evolution of newer groups during this period is very limited as concentration centers on the diversification and refinement of existing form, except for the microbe and insect who evolve in constant, changing variety, for they, as the sea are the Atom's workshops of animate continuity.

(The great benefit of these two orders, man has failed to define, as major research is directed toward wanton destruction of friend and foe alike, through poison, chemical spray and drugs. It would serve man well to conduct a thorough study of these fields, enabling an establishment of complete balance through biological control and due to the prolific nature and high energy value of certain specie of both insect and microorganism, an unlimited and as yet untapped source of food supplement is presented.

(There is tendency in man to forget that an exterminated specie will never reappear and improved methods of fishery, detection systems and deep-sea trawlers, combining with ever widening sources of pollution, are subjecting the denizens of the deep to the same merciless decimation as suffered by the unfortunate creatures of land and air through the firearm, chemical and high explosives. NECESSITY in man's probable span of existence does not tolerate allowance for the appearance of newer forms in a slow process of evolution.)

- Excerpt #7 from letter #6 -

Today, after an interminable quest and through your own research of the Atom, you have reached the culmination of a first stage in the mathematical fundamentals of this research, but as this factual science moves forward, it is absolutely disconnected from, dare not invade, the erroneous doctrines of theory, rooted only in the shadow world of your dark ages and which still completely dominates the social course of a planet.

Heretofore power, prestige, wealth, were usually subservient to God-Head, Pharoah, Priest, Religious Hierarchy or combination thereof, but with the advent of the Industrial Revolution the only truly monotheistic God, ever created by man, materialized in a symbolization of its Dollar Sign, whose worship now dictates every thought, deed, reaction, of all nations, creeds, organizations and individuals of earth. It is difficult to ascertain the ultimate destiny of a race, as it struggles under this self induced web of ambiguity, in the paradoxical maze that straddles half worlds of hallucination and materialism.

Your present success in achievements of science should herald symphonies of joy that resound throughout the world, but the reverberation is only the din of battle, the anguished cries of carnage, for the benefit to a social science, from the combined brain of all earth's scientists, are only crumbs that drop from the main theme of conquest as the greater knowledge of all becomes harnesses to Death with the latent evils of the Laser, of Chemical and Biological mediums being thoroughly explored, for their adaption to a degradation of war.

This continual refinement, in means to slaughter implants an insatiable urge, that inhibits the planet as chaos, violence and anarchy, re-echo the Uhuru of the African, in the melee of race riots, the crime waves, the unbalancing influence of dictatorial powers within democratic framework, in the Russian purges, fermentation of revolution and cold war, the thickening jungle of South America, the bomb of China, the belligerent Indonesian and many others, with dreams of their itchy fingers on the triggers of atomic destruction and the bloody dilemma of Vietnam, with a smoldering fuse that may shatter a planet, as Buddhist goads Buddhist, Catholic impinges Buddhist and government topples government in a feuding wilderness with the Great Powers pulling the strings of these performing puppets and to add to an insanity, the Montagnard tribesmen blithely ties an innocent buffalo to a stake and with inhuman brutality, methodically proceeds to hamstring, mutilate and torture it to death in sacrificial ritual depicting just one of the myriad diversified attributes to the myth of divinity in its senseless depravity.

- Excerpt #8 from letter #6 -

The wildest scope of imagination could not construe that this encompassing behavior represents even a step stage to intellectual advance of human culture and if indication of many thousands of years of repetition, although so unbelievable, may yet hold true, must a conclusion be drawn that the Atom in its refinement and endowment of the Brain to this Higher mammal has failed to omit or at least temper its essence of adversity that has been so evident in the predatory habit of the brute forms of preceding earth species, as to become inextricably entangled with all thought process? It is most incredible that a planet of such exquisite beauty and overall abundance could spawn its animals in this uncomplimentary mold of viciousness.

The original intent of debate was a thought of instilling a wider comprehension regarding Cosmic and Specie origin, its adverse and paradoxical composition, solely to influence your own intelligence in circumventing the pitfalls of unstable law that will beset an advancing entity as he struggles under the dilemma of tradition versus truth and to awaken a concept of relative equality to all creation as you approach a realm of Scientific Society and we fervently hope that at some stage along the line, just plain common sense will eventually become the gyro in the spiralling scope of war potential. It must be realistically clear as man, once again, contrives to fashion an extreme of nature into weapons of conquest and slaughter, that we returned to a scene of action that parallels, in principle and pattern, the period just prior to our bitter experience of a deadly exit from this same planet, so long ago.

Although, at present, we are not the intended targets, we did take advantage of a time element and the liberty of establishing a series of safeguards, should man of planet earth again go off the deep end. We are concentrating on a refinement in these checks that entails in simple explanation, a Magnetic Drain-Off and there is remote possibility that a temporary power failure could develop in isolated areas of very high electrical energy distribution and if, by chance, this condition ever becomes manifest there is no cause for alarm for it will be harmless to both equipment and personnel. It is regrettable that the energizing, on February 11, 1958 of our main neutralizing screen instituted a certain minor hardship, to some of your world's inhabitants, due to an almost negligible deflection of sun-energy and deviation of high altitude wind currents, but combining, through Radiation buildup with a minus diffusion factor of Meteor Dust which is the nuclei of water droplets, a very minor shift of storm tracks, rain and temperature patterns did occur. But the bomb left no alternative, to these precautionary measures, for lack of logic in testing and refinement and/or the probable irrational proliferation in the advent of actual warfare, could have triggered forces or devastation far beyond all human control.

No doubt, an attitude of the Scolding Mother permeates the conveyance of this series of letters, even though conceived in the humility of knowledge, but if they can accomplish the imprinting of one beneficial thought, a single step in the direction of a broader based philosophy and the force of review, minimize a force of arms, this effort may not become dedicated to the realm of wasted time.

P.S. End of series and this medium of limited contact.

By will of their ruling council, this last letter did end the possibility of any future personal attempt by the 100 strangers from space, even though in anonymous vein, to impart the urgent need of clearer understanding in the role that human intelligence should play in the scheme of Universal motivation. The fact that you are reading this book must instill an awareness that the thought does persist.

In full realization of—shall I say—the extremely tenuous position that they have occupied since 1904 in our ever expanding population, perhaps their words, related by men of Earth such as I, may give a little substance in awakening our world to the vital necessity of formulating international politics under policies of benefit, tempered by compassion, as envisioned by their ancestors so long ago.

It was compassion that prompted their mission to determine the path that we may pursue when the probing of our science would eventually disclose the tremendous power of Cosmic Energy. In 1937 the small group, in Germany, discovered that experiments were being conducted with the atom. This information set in motion a National effort of colossal proportion to isolate or localize the physical destruction of any device that may be born of nuclear research. The undertaking, spanning the time period of twenty years, culminated in 1958 with the activation of a world encompassing neutralizer; to party or nullify the many unpredictable phases of runaway chain reaction.

These long years of determinative investigation and intimate association with Earth's races also revealed the strange traits and critical fallacies that focus on one glaring deficiency in the social structures of all evolving civilization through the 10,000 years that has led to our present station of modern man.

Our progress, during these centuries, leaves a sharply defined trail of wanton waste and plunder of a planet's economic essentials of balance that had established an organization of interdependence between all living entities and their environment—an irrevocable Law of Nature, if it is to survive.

A deep study of Ecology, or application of its science to the doctrines of past and present Man Made Law, is non-existent. Man's law is designed only to satisfy the lust of selfish benefit, conceived under erroneous presumption that he was created from a special clay, accompanied by divine privileges of domination over all other matter. So, in thoughtless abandon he exercised a God given right to maim, slaughter, and destroy, in reshaping an environment to his own desire with its many sadistic channels and a now multiplying population, beyond even the realm of common sense. The analysis of documentary evidence exposes this great flaw as a continuous, widening rift that must inevitably crumble the foundation on which all life exists.

Actually, what is man of Earth? Merely a refined animal? Hardly!! Yet in essence, he did branch from a lower animal and, by so doing retained a similarity of organs and reproductive process. This dominant pattern, in the organization of organs and reproduction, has come down through the ages in all major orders of reptile, mammal, and Man. Whether a specie emerged on all four legs or with two arms and two legs from an egg hatched externally by heat of the sun, incubated by a parent or within the body of an entity, the basic is unchanged, with just an occasional modification in method. But, here the similarity between intellectual Man and the myriad other members of the Animal Kingdom ends.

Before the advent of a dominant Man, all animals, and the entire conglomerate of plant forms were dependent children to their great mother, Nature. Their destinies, in each given era, rigidly controlled by the economics of planetary law that evolves in a state of absolute equilibrium with air, mountain, land, desert and water. However, this complete balance, between an existing form and their habitat, is periodically upset as the mechanics of the galaxy's rotation are strongly influenced by a differential of constant to the Universal Nucleus.

The resulting intermittent climatic and surface changes on our planet do trigger the extinction of certain living orders, when the forces of this differential drastically alter an environment by pulling convection currents in its mantle through the static crust of Earth to raise up its mountain ranges. Temperature oscillation robs a good deal of water from the seas in building extensive ice fields and glaciers. But in turn, with the slow revolution of the galaxy, they will again melt to redistribute this precious fluid over land and sea that had been locked up as ice.

The mountains, even of today, are beginning to erode into the eventuality of low laying hills that will characterize the Earth's landscape some 60 million years in the future. These eras, as you must realize, cover tremendous spans of time during the Galaxy's 223 million year period of rotation and although there is a considerable amount of gas released or squeezed from a planet's interior and a residue of rock, soil, plant and animal remains, in the wake of these upheavals, it is essentially pure and will soon recycle in an adaptation to the continuity of life. Each emerging specie has shown an improvement in structure or mental capacity over its predecessor.

The simplicity in this law of physics remained fairly consistent, on Earth, until a mere 13 thousand years ago when an order of steadily developing primate animals, Elemental Man, was abruptly transformed into Intelligent Man, with a rapid expansion of the Human Brain that catapulted this extremely primitive race of beings a million years into the future through an endowment of teaching and in minor influence, intermarriage, rather than in the slow refinement of evolution. A beginning of the first Unnatural era of a Solar Systems history that Zrets' ancestors unwittingly instigated. His present people term our extravagance of decimation A Great Assault against Earth.

The big question mark. How long can it endure? To fully understand the unimaginable length of time compared to human life span that it has taken the atoms to assemble our Sun and through synthesis the elements of planets, and the atoms of Earth to evolve its plants, animals and composite that we know as the higher brain, one must visualize a gigantic swirling cloud of basic hydrogen gas and dust entailing several billion years in primary formation before it stabilized in the organization of our Solar System, five billion years ago.

In a broad and very brief analysis of principle, the core of this gas cloud, through gravitational force, tremendous energy pressure and friction compressed into our Sun, an atomic furnace a million miles in diameter fueled by a proton-proton fusion of hydrogen nuclei converting to helium in a central temperature of 20 million degrees. In this inferno of heat and pressure hydrogen atoms are stripped of their attendant electrons, leaving the naked protons. In the first step of the fusion cycle two protons collide to form the hydrogen isotope, deuterium with one proton and one neutron.

The impact causes two particles to fly out, one a neutrino, having no charge, passes completely through the sun and into the void of space. The other a positron that immediately meets an electron of negative charge and the two opposites proceed to annihilate each other.

In the second step the deuterium nucleus envelops another proton to evolve a new element, the isotope Helium 3, with two protons and one neutron. This violent seizure creates the radiant energy of gamma rays.

The final step of the cycle takes place when two helium 3 nuclei collide. This merger brings forth the stable nucleus of helium 4, two protons and two neutrons, as the collision jolts the two extra protons loose and they continue their way, to perhaps start the cycle over again or to combine the formation of other atoms in the synthesis of new elements. The remaining gas of the cloud, beyond the new Sun's perimeter is affected by the out pouring of its radiation and starts moving outward. As it moves away it is also losing heat and breaks into spinning globular entities while assimilating helium, silica, oxygen, carbon, nitrogen, etc., from this energy flux.

Oxygen, combining with silica and dust, create the initial cores of their gravitation fields, but as they did not attain the required temperature of a fusion cycle, eventually compressed into the planets that we know as Mercury, Venus, Earth, Mars and Planet X, the pulverized planet that originally orbited between Mars and Jupiter. The outer nebulous planets lost too much heat, in the chill of outer space and were unable to generate the energy to combine rock, iron, magnesium etc., into a completely solidified structure.

They spin today, partially solidified giants of chemical gas and ice, without a great deal of compression from the size of their primary globes. But regardless of size or composition, all circle in specific orbits of formulation, their parent—The Sun!

As this story basically concerns Earth, we will follow its development after the nebulous proto planet had compressed from the inward pulling force of its gravitational field and again building heat energy from this contraction, plus that of radioactivity in the complex reaction of combining chemical compounds into a solidified matter, began its cycle.

During the next one billion years many changes occurred, as oxygen combining with Silica created the myriad oxides and Rock of Earth's forming mantle. Hydrogen, the major gas of its atmosphere, combined with oxygen to form water that rained down on this seething, growing sphere and in the beginning only vaporized. Hydrogen, uniting with nitrogen created vast clouds of ammonia and with carbon, to bring methane into being.

These three gases, Hydrogen and the compound gases Ammonia and Methane, with a smaller percentage of the inert gases Helium, Neon and Argon formed the primeval atmosphere of our evolving planet.

As the cycle of formation continued, heat energy was also responsible for a synthesis of ammonia and methane into amino acids, a radical chemical water vapor and carbon dioxide to combine with the water of the hydrogen-oxygen union in an incessant pelting of a solidifying crust. Near the end of this billion year period, abetted by the icy breath of the nucleus, as the galaxy's arm positioned it at High Noon a sufficient cooling allowed a water build up and the infant planet Earth started its way to maturity, a solidified sphere, covered with a worldwide shallow sea of boiling water.

In arriving at this planet of steaming atmosphere and water, the long conversion sequence of chemical solution and compound used all the free oxygen and the category that we know as life was not present. The process of a hardening crust, covered with water, also sealed the intense heat and gas of the planet's interior and as it had to vent or explode, relief valves, in the form of volcanos, began thrusting their crests above the seas' surface and the upwelling of gas, lava, magma and igneous granitic rock spread over the sea beds to institute the foundation of continental platforms.

In the following half billion years, or roughly the space of two galactic revolutions, the duplication of the mantles convection cells being pulled through the crust, as mountains, combining with lava flows and their inevitable erosion by oxidation, running water and grinding ice of glacial movement slowly established the composite igneous and sedimentary rock shields of Earth's present continents.

An inconceivable geological time span of three and a half billion years has since passed as the spreading of growing continents raised the water levels to deepen the oceans, but in the warm shallows of ancient seas, Amino acids through hydrolysis, created the nucleic acids of budding plant life, Bacteria, Fungi, and Blue-green Algae. These microscopic plants, needing food to survive formed carbohydrates from water, carbon dioxide and sun energy that left a by-product of free oxygen to mix with the sea water. This reaction established a suitable environment for the adaptation of future animal life and from the arrest of certain Algae spoor, an Amoeba was born, the inceptive of a gradual animal evolution.

The ensuing eons witnessed the arrival of protozoans, sponges, anemone, half plant-half animal. Then an endless parade of jelly fish, corals, trilobites, molluscs, tunicate, Crustacea and fish of the sea. Four hundred and fifty million years ago the first plants washed up on the barren rock of a shoreline and in a symbiotic association of fungi and primitive Algae Moss, the plant kingdom gained a foothold on land. The Liverwort followed and as it developed, scorpions and spiders ventured ashore. Amphibians divided their time between land and sea, tetrapods appear and evolution of the anapsid and synapsid orders of reptile began to definitely break the complete animal dependency on a water habitat. The diapsid later branched from the anapsid, to father Lizards, Dinosaurs, Birds, Snakes, etc. The diversifying Synapsid brought Marsupials and Mammals to life.

Sixty million years have now passed since The Atom started an amazing sequence of evolutionary legerdemain with a small squirrel-like animal that lived in the trees. Contrary to the majority of its contemporaries, this little mammal hunted with its eyes, rather than by scent and utilized its hand-like front appendages in picking berries or to grub for insects, in lieu of the fang to seize its food. These traits were about the only thing in common between the primate and the strange associated links that led to an ultimate end product —"Man."

In 20 million years the Lemur and spreading Monkey clan had evolved but their forward progress stopped after reaching the station of completed entities. Another tendril shoots out from this many branched symbolic vine and 10 million years later the Gibbon gives impetus to a procession of aberrant Apes that also came to a dead-end in the brain of the chimpanzee, the peak of Ape evolution and a few peculiarities are evident. The animal tail disappeared.

A semi-upright stance was achieved, but fully erect posture and exclusive bipedal gait was not consummated. The quality of ingenuity, in coordination of hand and brain was sadly lacking. Although the hands and arms were used extensively in daily routine, the Ape family remain basic quadrupedal animals. (In the time of Zret's ancestors, on our planet, a great wealth of fossils and very ancient rock strata was available for study. Information in this book has been translated, by Zret from records of research conducted in these fields 12,800 years ago.)

The determination of the Atom to personify itself in the vehicle of a Brain came a step closer to fruition with the last branching of the Primate line.

In opening this powerful drama, the stage is set in three scenes, comprising the island continents of Atlantis and Lemuria destined to be destroyed by a race originating in the third scene—Africa. The appearance of the initial five characters in this drama, with exception to the second and third, were spaced 500 thousand years apart. The significance of this even spacing could not be determined by research, but it did have a definite influence on the mental capacity of their evolving races.

The curtain first raises 16 million years ago in the forests of Southern Atlantis. It is now a fabled land, but even then it had an air of the unreal. Massive black mountains, glistening in the sun, with wisps of smoke curling skyward from a few still active volcanic cones, whose lava and upwelling melanochroic rock had built this part of the Island in a distant past. The chemical Melanin was also an overly active ingredient in the tissue of plant and animal, responsible for abnormally dark hues. Red blossoms and deep green leaves predominate the foliage.

As we look around, through the eyes of research, a group of small animals catches the eye. Some scampering in the trees and others walking on the ground, grabbing at berries or scratching for roots. At first glance they appear to be a family of Chimpanzees, but close scrutiny immediately reveals several conflicting traits: those on the ground are walking upright on two feet and although they have a slight crouch and sway a bit from side to side, the dangling arms are NOT used as accessories to quadruped gait. You are now looking at a brand new entity, a Hominid, the first erect bipedal elemental Human of planet Earth.

An initiation to evolution of the Human Race

An examination of the fossil clearly shows the drastic changes in skeletal structure between supporting the weight and organs in vertical posture, as opposed to horizontal positioning in the quadruped.

At this early date the feet had modified only slightly from the purely grasping toes of an ape. The leg and hip bones were straight. The pelvis had shortened and broadened with a stiffened spine and reshaped rib cage. The foramen magnum hole in the skull through which pass the nerves from the spinal column to the pituitary gland and brain, was now almost directly down from the top of the skull as opposed to one nearer the back of the head in an animal.

The number of teeth in Ape and Hominid were the same, but shape of the jaw bones changed. In the Ape it is a U with equal spacing between front and back molars. The Hominids jaw bones splay out toward the back of the mouth causing the rear molars to space further apart than those in front. The roof of the mouth had also arched. This basic structure has been constant in the evolution of all succeeding Earth Races. Melanin remained the prime factor of determination of pigmentation of eyes and hair, but inorganic compounds of environment in water and food did stain skin pigmentation in the varying colors of each race as it evolved. The line of Pro Consul, which earlier had evolved the Gorilla and Chimpanzee was also the branching factor to bring the Hominids into being.

500 thousand years later and thousands of miles apart, on beautiful Northern Atlantis and Lemuria, two races appeared simultaneously: the Blue on Atlantis, the Red on Lemuria. Skin pigmentation being influenced respectively, by iron sulphide and iron oxide. The incipient of the Blue race was an exception in size, six feet tall, as compared with three to four feet tall of all other budding races.

Another half million years roll by to an emergence of Homo Sapiens in Africa and Lemuria completing the cycle, 144 million years ago in the last and higher evolution of a Hominid, the primal ancestor of the Golden race.

In the long interim that led to a period 13 thousand years before present these races became taller, more robust through the exceedingly slow and tedious process of natural evolution, who at this point had only attained a low level of community life, in the status of hunters. Their weapons simulated the fang and claw of the predator in an obvious method of tying chipped stones to short sticks for axes and to longer ones for thrusting spears. (An improvement over pointed sticks).

A few implements of fine, flaked stone were in common use that represented an ultimate of development. Ingenuity in the fashioning of even simple mechanical devices, such as the bow and arrow, was not achieved. The organization of tribal law was also beyond the scope of a social science still influenced by ancestral instinct of herding, as the stronger Bull ruled his herd in a way of life solely dependent on the abundance of game. Superstition produced a certain art that pictured these animals on the walls of dark caves in a thought of imprisoning the spirit, thereby holding it close to a specific locale and accessible to slaughter. This initial use of mysticism by man in an attempt at control of an environment was the root of later evolving ritual that has taken such command of the human mind.

Over this strange planet of exotic beauty and conflicting contrast of viciousness, a unique machine of an alien race hovers. It seems suspended in an air of breathless anticipation, then slowly descends, three legs swing out in position on its bottom and the first Flying Saucer touches down on Earth. Snapping electronic flashes arc to the pad at the base of each leg, all becomes silence as it rest motionless in a small flowering meadow. From the craft's center a ramp slips toward the ground and a lone individual walks down into the sunlight.

A human being of very fair skin, blue eyes, and as the breeze ruffles his hair it glistens as gold, in the Sun. He strolls about, looking, evaluating, then presses a button on a panel at his chest to summon 29 companions from the ship. They hug each other, as tears of joy dampen their faces, for the racial quest of a dream that had started so many millenniums before, on a planet of a distant solar system, had finally culminated in Paradise.

The dream however lasted less than 300 years, as the tremendous knowledge they had endowed to the wild, primitive populations of Earth, broke their balance of natural development and without the refinement of perhaps a million evolutionary years, they were catapulted into the far flung reaches of science with catastrophic result. The device that had proven so advantageous to the people of outer space in a study of stratigraphy and removal of fossils embedded in this rock, was converted into the first sophisticated weapon by men of Earth. Five billion years of the planet's history almost came to an end in one day by the brain of early man impregnated with knowledge, yet maintaining the inherent traits of animalistic viciousness and predation.

We, the descendents of these same multicolored races,

are still in a chaotic state of constant conflict with ourselves and nature. World wide politicracy is not guided by the science of balance, but a runaway explosion, spurred on by the veiled ritual of ancient pagan fertility cults.

Chemistry and the blast of a nuclear bomb is instantaneous death to many in an immediate vicinity and adds its quota to the steady stream of pollutants, pouring into a suffering atmosphere from our use of fossil fuels. Soil and water do not escape the poisons of industrial acids or the ever swelling mass of population wastes that are spreading over land and sea.

Atoms for Peace, according to my friend Zret, is a misnomer, for there is little likelihood of a Peaceful atom, once man has tampered with its structure. The debris of utilization only adding its special menace to the gigantic trash heap that cannot be recycled into a benefit of living matter. Man MUST, at least, temper his greed and the homage demanded by its avaricious god of profit. The highest priority on the planet today is a need of a complete study of Ecology by all the world's brilliant scientists and analysis of their findings acted on immediately, regardless of cost. Without an absolute understanding of the part a human brain should play in its role of a symbolic pendulum regulating the entire environment, it may disappear in the flash of fusing atoms or to succumb through the insidious creeping death of unbalanced nature. Either eventuality will leave the great arsenals and sprawling factories rusting away on a desolate landscape as the planet Earth becomes a contemporary of its barren, lifeless satellite - THE MOON.

In the simplicity of love many miracles are born but only through compassion of a human brain may they flower in the beauty of Universal Brotherhood.

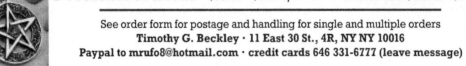

Printed in Great Britain
by Amazon

85517469R00099